PRAISE FOR
— Things My Mama Never Told Me —

"Nancy Johnson's new book, *Things My Mama Never Told Me*, is a gift to teenagers and mothers of teenage girls everywhere. Pick a subject a teen girl may be struggling with and it's in there. But what truly makes the book so special is Nancy's warm voice guiding you along the way. She gets the struggle and is there to take you by the hand and walk you through some of the toughest issues you may face. It's like having a teen life coach by your side offering the facts, giving you perspective, and cheering you on. It's brilliant."

—Marni Freedman, LMFT, Former Therapist for Youth at Risk
author of 7 Essential Tools (2016) and Permission to Roar for
Female Thought Leaders (2018)

"Nancy Mae Johnson's *Things My Mama Never Told Me* is the teen *Our Bodies, Ourselves* for the 21st century, offering a path to wholeness for teen girls facing coming of age. I can't wait to bring *Things My Mama Never Told Me* into my home, not only for my teenagers (sons and daughter alike), but for my teen self."

—Tania Pryputniewicz,
author of *November Butterfly* (2014, Saddle Road Press) and
Heart's Compass Tarot (2021, Two Fine Crows Books)

"I wish every tween girl could take a course in school with *Things My Mama Never Told Me* as the main text and was given her very own copy to have as reference for years to follow. I will happily hand this sensitive, direct, honest book to my own daughters who are in their twenties, and give copies to my colleagues for their offices. It's a must-have."

—Franciene Alexa Lehmann, Ph.D., School Psychologist

"Nancy Johnson, affectionately known as Mrs. J, was an intrigue factor in the transformation of Hoover High School. From day one, she understood the need for students to see and feel her "heart" as she demanded their best efforts. How fitting it is for her to share these life stories. Her writings will tug at your heart as they present clear insights into the lives of today's young people."

—Doug Williams, Past Principal, Hoover HS San Diego

"During Nancy Johnson's 20 years at Hoover HS, she reached out to students emotionally and socially as well as academically. We are honored that she returned to Hoover to interview students for *Things My Mama Never Told Me*, and look forward to her continued work in the schools sharing her book with teen girls in small group or whole class settings."

—Jason Babineau, Current Principal, Hoover HS, San Diego
—Chuck Podhorsky, Principal, La Jolla HS, San Diego

"As a student teacher just beginning my career, I learned invaluable lessons from Nancy Johnson. She is a master at getting teenagers to reflect on their own lives in relationship to moving storylines and deep themes. This book takes on the most relevant and pressing topics our youth are already thinking about. It will grip you and move you to cheer for the young people in your own circle."

—Justin Phillips, Walker Elementary, San Diego

"Finally, a book that is, essentially, a candid conversation with young women about the subjects they care most about and yet get the least guidance from adults. Johnson is honest and vulnerable and allows for her readers to be as well. The interviews, information, and suggested follow-up tasks are essential for any young woman."

—Valerie Woodfill, English teacher, Hoover HS, San Diego
Academy of Health and Healthier Communities *partnered with Children's Hospital FACES for the Future.*

"I am thankful that Mrs. J chose me to be part of her journey as an author. My hopes are that readers will begin to see how key things that Mrs. Johnson addresses are so very important in understanding their teen years and that this book will bring about positive change in their lives."

—Adrian, student interviewee

"I was a junior in high school when Mrs. Johnson interviewed me for her book, *Things My Mama Never Told Me*. I shared my story because I knew it could potentially help others. I would have really benefited from having something like this to help me as I grew up."

—Jessica, student interviewee

THINGS MY MAMA NEVER TOLD ME

A FUNNY AND SOMETIMES SERIOUS GUIDE FOR TEEN GIRLS AND THE PEOPLE WHO LOVE THEM

by

Nancy Mae Johnson

FROM THE TINY ACORN ...
GROWS THE MIGHTY OAK

This is a work of nonfiction. Names have been changed to protect the anonymity of interviewees. Stories and interviews have been told to the best of the author's ability and memory.

Things My Mama Never Told Me

For information, address Acorn Publishing, LLC, 3943 Irvine Blvd. Ste. 218, Irvine, CA 92602
www.acornpublishingllc.com

Cover design by Damonza.com with thanks to Lindsey Salatka

Author photo by Holly Rone Photography; hollyronephotography.com

Interior design and digital formatting by Debra Cranfield Kennedy

ISBN—978-1-952112-39-3
Library of Congress Control Number: 2021901458

Dedicated To

MY DAUGHTERS
Nicole, Holly, and Jolene

MY GRANDDAUGHTERS
Nora, Taylor, Sophia, and Georgia

MY SISTERS
Peggy, Cynthia, Julie, and Peggy A.

MY NIECES
*Leyna, Hannah N, Lindsay, Sandy,
Hannah J, Tina, Michelle, and Gina*

MY STUDENTS

AND . . . *All the other amazing women in my life*

In Memory Of

MY MOTHER
Mary Lou Farness

MY MOTHER-IN-LAW
Barbara Lois Johnson

MY GRANDMOTHERS
Esther Farness and May Riddle

MY FRIEND
Carole Prewett

Table of Contents

THINGS

MY MAMA

NEVER

TOLD ME

A note to those who don't have a mama...

My dear friend, Madonna Treadway, lost her parents when she was a young child. She wrote a book out of that experience called Six Healing Questions: A Gentle Path to Facing Childhood Loss of a Parent. She reminded me that she didn't have a mama to teach her things or to talk with while reading this book. Like my friend Madonna, you might also be reading this without a mama in your life. Know that, first and foremost, this book is for you. But if you have an aunt, grandma, sister, mentor, or even best friend who means a lot to you, invite her to join you in this process. I believe that every woman would benefit in healing her teen self. And if you are close to your dad or another male figure, let's challenge those gender roles we will talk about soon. Follow your intuition and find a safe, healthy person with whom to explore these issues.

A note to adult women reading this book...

It's never too late to heal your teen self. I am a living testament... and I'm not done yet.

I hope that in reading this book you will receive a sense for how powerful and worthy of compassion you are. I hope that you will commune with your teen self and help her reveal the secrets and shame that she holds within. I hope that you forgive her and cry with her over bad decisions she made at her own expense.

I hope you see the power you give yourself when you take care of you first and hold more compassion for you than for any other person. As you set new boundaries for yourself, I hope you focus on you, and set standards of conduct for your own emotional, physical, and mental health regardless of another person's reaction. I hope through self-care and forgiveness, you will have more energy and strength to be the best version of yourself for those you love and with whom you want to share your life.

A note to everyone . . .

I hope that this book has landed in your hands at exactly the right moment for you.

If you are a teen, this book is for you. It will give you answers to questions you may be too uncomfortable to ask. It will give you the option to put words to your fears or share secrets with a safe person. It's when we bring our worries, questions, fears, and secrets into the light that we can find comfort and serenity.

If you are a woman, whether a mama or not, this book is for you. It will give you the opportunity to revisit some old wounds and find some love and forgiveness for your teen self.

Whoever you are today, and whatever mistakes you may have made before today, you are not alone. You are the first to hear the stories I was not brave enough to tell my mama. I hope that you will find a safe, loving person with whom to share some of your stories. I hope that you and your teen self will be able to release some of the confusion, anger, or pain you may be holding inside.

The teen girls I interviewed for this book were and are brave, resilient, powerful women just like you. Despite their own sometimes overwhelming and scary circumstances, they overcame their fears and held onto their dreams with unwavering strength.

Chapter 1

Body Image & Self-Esteem

Can you remember where you got your first ideas about what your body should look like? Was it from social media? Videos? TV? Movies? Magazines? Your peers? How old were you when you stopped spinning in your tutu or making funny faces at yourself in front of the mirror?

Now that you're older, have you ever locked the bathroom door to take your shower and afterwards wiped the steamy mirror to reveal the body that is never going to be perfect enough? Maybe you think your forehead is too big, your eyes are too far apart, your nose is too long or too wide, your lips are too skinny or too full. As your eyes move to your breasts, you can't believe how flat or fat or droopy they are . . . and you're grateful the mirror is not full length?

When did we stop looking at ourselves with sheer joy and silliness and start looking at our bodies with a critical eye? More importantly, why? Why do we let images affect our self-esteem? Why do we let expectations affect how we feel about ourselves? The answers to these questions are important because we are important. Because body image and self-esteem go hand-in-hand. Only in developing our unique image and style can we find joy and esteem for ourselves. Self-esteem is developing our abilities and worth so that we can fully embrace the beautiful, perfect reflection in the mirror.

My Story

Beginning in middle school, the education about body parts and their functions that I valued—and I'm not proud of this looking back—came from the girls in gym class. I watched and listened to my peers, and formulated my first opinions about my body image and my self-worth from them. This self-evaluation was made easier by the fact that mandatory showers started in middle school and continued throughout high school.

I was skinny and had small breasts. I was very shy about my body and wrapped the small, school-issued towel around me the best I could to get in line for the showers. I got in and out as fast as I could, keeping my back to the shower opening. I was a Houdini dresser like many of the girls. Barely dry off. Keep your back to the narrow rows of silver lockers. Eyes down, always down. Don't make eye contact with anyone. Slip on your underwear quickly. Clasp your bra in the front and whip that baby around quickly to cover those tiny Hershey's kisses.

By the time I got to high school, I had learned to cover up my still-present insecurities about my body and my nakedness with attitude. I adopted either a "none of it matters" attitude or an "isn't it all hilarious attitude" that was sometimes tough and sometimes funny. Underneath my bravado and my humor, I was still a little mortified.

Gym class conversations in high school became more detailed and intimate. They centered on boys: how we should dress for boys, what we should do for boys, what boys like. Indirectly, though, we were getting messages about ourselves: girls are not as important as boys, boys' feelings and needs should be protected, girls should please boys. On rainy days, we didn't dress out, gathering instead in the gymnasium or one of the dance rooms. Girls sat along the perimeter of the room, backs leaning against the walls. Because all grade levels were in gym together, many of the stories were far above my freshman experience. One day, as I sat staring at the textbook I was studying for my next class, a few girls sitting close by began to talk:

"Dan and I went out last night. It was dreamy. His sweet lips make me crazy. I let him slip his hand under my shirt."

"I told Mike he could give me a hickey necklace. He wanted to show me off to his friends."

"Are you guys going to go all the way?"

"Probably. We both want to. I'm trying to go a little slow after Sam. He ended up being such a jerk."

"Hey, did you see Janet at the game Friday night? I would have been so embarrassed. She looked like a cow in that outfit; she obviously has had a few two many Twinkies lately. Can we say diet pills?"

"God, I know. There should be some kind of rule about how fat you can be to be a cheerleader. Plus, John is the quarterback! He's not going to put up with that!"

I stayed incognito in my very interesting textbook, but I was getting a different kind of education about what I should look like and what boys wanted. If I didn't look like these student instructors or think like them or have the same worldly experiences, maybe I would never be accepted or popular or liked by a boy. I knew intellectually that I didn't have to agree with them or be like them, but emotionally they could play havoc with my feelings and my expectations for myself.

Your Story

Many things have changed since I was in high school in the '70s, and yet some things haven't changed at all. I read hundreds of journal entries when I was a high school teacher and interviewed many girls at local San Diego high schools during the writing of this book. Girls still compare themselves to, feel embarrassed by, and wish they looked like someone else. They still pick up body, clothes, and hair trends from movie stars, models, and singing sensations. Whatever the new norm is in each generation, that is often the look girls want to have. Teen girls today not only hear from other girls what is acceptable for their own bodies, but they learn from YouTube and social media—not always reliable sources.

These amazing girls confirmed my own YouTube, internet, and social media research: Strong is the new skinny. Butts are good. In J.Lo's generation, she struggled with her big butt, but today butts are in—probably in part thanks to her. Girls even want butt implants. Full-figured models are new to the 21st century. Still, magazine shots are not necessarily realistic when we compare a Cosmopolitan magazine glamour shot to a movie-star-caught-in-a-gossip-magazine shot. Facelifts and cosmetic surgery are pretty common in more affluent circles. Apparently, it's the new rage to wear the same kind of corsets that women wore way back in the day so that waists look tiny and breasts and butts look ample.

While we're talking about breasts, I talked to a sixteen-year-old girl named Isabel who we'll hear more from in a bit about body image and self-esteem in general. She shared this story:

I have the most trouble with breast size. I bought this dress to wear to a special event. I couldn't wear a normal bra because of the style. I looked online to see what I might be able to do. I read about "taping boobs to make them look bigger and fuller." I tried the technique and wore the dress that night with the tape tightly holding my boobs closer together than normal so they would look bigger without wearing a regular bra.

I still have the marks the tape left below my breasts. When I see them, I remember the time I tried to do something that was artificial because I wanted to look like and be like something or someone else. When I look back on the journey of developing, I know now that I don't want to harm my body just to look a certain way. I don't want to feel good by not feeling good. I want to accept my breasts as they are.

I'm shopping for a dress right now for an important school dance. I'm still trying to appreciate and accept the way my body looks. Cleavage? No. I may just look flatter. I want to try the dresses on, and then look in the mirror and say, "I feel good about myself because I'm beautiful, not because my boobs are beautiful."

Did You Know / Fun Facts

Self-Esteem

Self-esteem is your belief that you have worth, that you are proud of yourself and will contribute positively to society.

The "esteem" part of self-esteem comes from the Latin verb *aestimāre*, meaning to value, so think of self-esteem as how you value yourself.

We all have low self-esteem sometimes. That's normal.

When we have long periods of time when our low self-esteem takes over, we may be depressed. It may be time to seek some help from someone we trust and/or a professional. In some circumstances, we need medication because our natural levels of serotonin are low. (Serotonin is the chemical in our brains that makes us happy.) We will talk more about stress and keeping healthy in **Chapter 6**.

Body Image Viewpoints from Teens of Different Cultures

In my recent interviews with students from local high schools, I've learned that beauty is different depending on the culture or ethnicity with which a girl connects. Light-skinned and light-haired girls want to spend summer days at the beach getting tans. The teen girls who come to my home on exchange programs from China, Japan, Korea, and Thailand cover up completely when they go out in the sun because dark skin is not considered beautiful in their countries. They want their skin to stay fair, soft, and wrinkle-free.

An insightful Iraqi student with deep brown eyes and a warm smile one day explained to me the reason she wears long dresses and skirts and a hijab covering her hair. It is not accepted in her culture for her to show her body or her hair.

"Young women should attract their partners with their personality and their intelligence; their bodies or hair should not factor into the equation." There is the added layer for Muslim women that goes beyond beauty because of the fear and stereotypes around any person who wears a hijab. Negative views of Muslim people are still prevalent simply because 9/11 terrorists were Muslim. This young woman not only has the normal teen insecurities about body image, she has the additional concern of being perceived with suspicion because of her culture.

For example, when news channels covered the war in Iraq, they often portrayed Muslims as the enemy. She told me, "My uncles and aunts and grandparents still live in Iraq, in the midst of war. My family here worries about them every day. We watch the news and see our neighborhoods on the screen. We pray that we will not see a familiar face amongst the wreckage and death." At school, she felt singled out, not only because of her dress but because of the judgment she perceived was directed to her and her family because of their culture.

Let's go back to Isabel who shared the story about breasts. She is a sophomore in high school who was born in Guatemala and adopted as a baby by her two Caucasian moms.

In our interview, I asked her several questions:

NANCY: *Do you think being from a different culture, or being adopted, or just looking different than your mothers has affected your self-image?*

ISABEL: **I don't really know how much of an impact my differences have had on me, if any. Sometimes I felt out of place as a young girl, but not ashamed. The friends I grew up with were all supportive and embraced diversity.**

I don't recall ever hearing negative comments from anyone about my appearance. My friends and I have always supported each other, cared about each other, and loved each other. We have never really had a conversation about it, but we just know.

NANCY: *When you think of emotions around body image, what do you think about?*

ISABEL: **Being short brings up some of those emotions of being different. About three years ago, I chipped a bone in my finger and had to have x-rays. My pediatrician came in and was looking at my growth chart. I had always been in the lowest fifteen percent of the population in terms of height, so I was used to being small. At the time, I was in the seventh grade and was four-foot-ten inches tall. I remember the conversation being a significant moment for me.**

We were meeting at Isabel's house, and she asked her mom to join us to help her remember the conversation. They remembered that the doctor said, "It looks like you've leveled off and you are done growing." Isabel remembered her mom looking completely shocked, and her mom agreed that she said, "What? Last time we saw you she was on a trajectory to be five-foot-three inches." Isabel said that her mom started to cry a little during the appointment. The doctor explained, "She's had her period for over a year and the x-rays show the growth plate closed." Isabel said, "I cried too after the doctor left. I didn't expect my mom to react like that."

Isabel excused her mom from the room, and we continued.

NANCY: *Why do you think that moment stood out for you so much if you had always been in the fifteenth percentile on the growth chart?*

ISABEL: **The moment stands out because it was the realization that I was being compared to thousands of children** all over the country. It solidified that I wasn't going to grow anymore. I had to say to myself, "This is how tall I'm going to be. I want to love and accept myself for who I am. I can't compare myself to apples. I'm an orange. If I need someone to reach the butter on the top shelf, I can ask for help.

This memory seemed to open up some feelings for Isabel that were a little different than those feelings of acceptance with which we opened the interview.

NANCY: *How did this incident help you accept who you are or affect your self-esteem?*

ISABEL: I've never liked the fact that I was adopted and from another culture. I put up a wall around myself and tried to separate myself from that part of me. The wall kept me from being unhappy about where I was from. I didn't want to learn Spanish. I didn't want to wear colorful clothes. It was hard and interesting and difficult.

NANCY: *What part of that wall made it the most difficult for you?*

ISABEL: I am an American. I eat American food and wear American clothes. I only spent ten months of my life in Guatemala. Those ten months do not define me. I was always trying to fit in with my very white mothers and very white cousins. Why would I want to wear colorful clothes and speak Spanish so that I could not fit in even more? Why should I be proud of being from a third world country? I thought it was bad to be seen as the Guatemalan girl.

NANCY: *How did those feelings translate to how you felt about yourself?*

ISABEL: It wasn't that I didn't love myself or didn't like the way I looked. It was the contrast between my black hair and brown skin and the blonde hair and white skin of my mothers, my aunts and uncles, and my cousins. Everyone else was tall and willowy. I loved different cultures and colors and countries, but I wanted to be European American like my family. I stuffed these feelings the best I could and built a wall to protect myself. I was self-conscious and didn't like that part of me.

NANCY: *How did this translate when you began your high school experience?*

ISABEL: When I was thinking about what language to take in high school, I didn't want to take Spanish. When my mom and I were talking about it, I got very angry and said, "I don't want to take Spanish. I don't know why. I just don't like it!" My mom said, "I think part of you not wanting to learn Spanish is you disliking that you are Latina and different from your adoptive family. You want to deny that part of you."

NANCY: *Did you think your mom was right?*

ISABEL: I didn't agree. I told her, "No! Why would I do that?" I thought to myself, "Why would my own mother think that I don't love myself?" I was very upset. My mom just said, "Okay. I just know that you feel like you don't fit in with the family, and this may be related." She knew from experience that when I got that upset, I didn't want to talk about it for a while. Looking back, she was and is right. I felt ashamed that I was adopted. I felt ashamed that I looked different.

NANCY: *Have those feelings changed for you during these last two high school years?*

ISABEL: Yes. I have a boyfriend now who helped me break down that wall. He is Mexican and embraces his culture and food. Since I've been with him, I have realized that it's okay to look different. I've started to accept that side of me. I tried to block out Spanish and that it was my language of origin. I was told it's okay to be different, but I never let it sink in.

NANCY: *Has this new relationship helped you accept yourself?*

ISABEL: I feel more comfortable now. I look like my boyfriend and his family. Guatemala is not Mexico, but it's in the same region. This knowledge helped me bring down the wall. Being around my boyfriend and his family, and already having done a lot of practice with self-love and self-acceptance, I feel better about myself. It has made me more curious about my birth family and exploring where I'm from. Being adopted is still difficult sometimes, but it feels a little easier to accept.

What I Wish My Mama Would Have Told Me

I wish my mama would have told me about the variety of personalities, body shapes, and maturation cycles that are special and specific to each individual. I wish she would have told me that sometimes teen girls judge each other and themselves, especially when it comes to bodies and outward appearance.

I wish she would have told me that seeing each other in gym class naked or half-dressed is not necessarily a bad thing, as long as we don't judge ourselves or find ourselves inadequate. What if, instead, we saw gym class as an amazing way to fight against the perfect teenager that lives only in our minds: tall, slender, beautiful, perfect boobs, acne-free, stretch-mark-free with every body part hand-crafted by some beautiful, perfect Superhero. There are a gazillion imperfections and perfections in every woman ever born. What a way to confirm that our friends—often influenced by unrealistic expectations—are wrong about their expectations.

I wish my mama would have told me that I was going to hear

stories about what I should think, what I should look like, and who I should be. I wish she would have told me to make some decisions about who I wanted to be and what I would or would not do *before* I was influenced by friends (or social media).

I wish my mama would have said, "There will probably be a million times when you will feel less than, because that's the nature of being a teen. Find a balance. Feel your pain. Share your pain. Laugh about your pain when you can. The more you share the pain, the more you'll be able to see the funny, sad, sick, lovely insanity of being a teenager. You are worthwhile and talented. You have something to share that is important. Value yourself and love yourself. You're awesome!"

Opportunities to Journal

* What messages do you get from friends about what you should look like, or how you should think? How do these messages make you feel?

* Explain a time you felt "less than" because you compared yourself to other girls.

* What messages do you get from social media about your body, your appearance, your choices? How do these messages affect your self-esteem? Do others sometimes influence the way you feel about yourself?

* How do you cope/hang on to who you really are?

Take-Aways

* Respect you have for your body, your abilities, and your worth work together to create self-esteem.

* Beware of getting information about body image from girls in gym class, YouTube, or social media. The information is likely to be wrong—or at the very least will make you feel bad about yourself.

* The definition of the perfect body will continue to change until

the end of time. It depends on the styles and constructs of the time, the ethnicity or culture a girl connects with, and even pop culture which is defined by movies, videos, and songs.

* Being adopted, especially if you are from another country than your adoptive family, can make you feel like an outsider. In the end, we learn that being different is a gift, and accepting yourself just as you are is the goal.

* Instead of comparing yourself to others and judging your inadequacies, know that there are a gazillion imperfections and perfections in every woman ever born.

* Own your beautiful body type. Don't compare yourself to apples if you're an orange!

Chapter 2

Hair & Peer Pressure

Do you ever feel pressure from your friends or your family to wear your hair a certain way? And I'm not just talking about the hair on your head. Do you have to fight for the right to wax, pluck, or shave in order to tame the hair on your brows, face, armpits, legs, fingers, toes, and . . . elsewhere? Once you find a look you like, do you still listen to remarks from your friends and feel pressure to change your look?

Peer pressure is often felt most when it comes to that body image we talked about in **Chapter 1**. Hair is a part of body image, and maybe it's a bit easier to control than factors like height or weight. Being "too tall or too short" is impossible to change. Being underweight or overweight is hard to change. But we can adjust what we see as our inadequacies with shoes, clothes, makeup, and hair. No matter what we do to create our own body image, we might still feel pressured by our peers to look and dress a certain way.

Your hair—and the hair you wish to do without—can cause anxiety and pressure. It's important to filter the information coming at you from all sides, decide what's right for you, and then negotiate with parents for the right to leave or take away body hair. In the end, explore for yourself why you make the decisions you do about hair, makeup, and clothes. Decide for yourself what look will define you.

My Story

When I was a baby—according to the pictures—it was all about my mother's magic fingers. She created a gentle swell on the top of my head with pink gel. By the time I was five, my swell had grown into long, thick locks that could be coaxed into banana curls. Every Saturday night, my mother's fingers wrapped the gel-doused strands of hair sideways around each pink, spongy curler before clipping the pseudo sausages close to my head. My mother would brush each curl around her fingers the following morning until I was a curly manifestation of girlhood.

Even though my father did not participate in the care of my hair, it was blatantly apparent from his own Elvis Presley flip, substantial sideburns, and the forest growing on his legs that Dad was the main source of my bountiful hair. When I was in elementary school, it was too early in my own development to feel the trepidation that would come later when I realized that his *genes* were my genes. Unless I wanted to wear *jeans* for the rest of my life, there was going to have to be some major reconstruction happening in my future. I was perfectly willing to consider wearing jeans over my black, lush forest of manly leg hair for the rest of my life, but by middle school there was the equally dark, nonfeminine hair that had sprouted up on my delicate arms and—scarier yet—under my armpits.

The girls in my sixth-grade class, with their baby-fine, white-yellow, so fresh and so clean body hair, budding breasts, and shapely, athletic arms, started wearing A-line dresses with scoop necks, flouncy skirts with sleeveless tops, and strappy, stylish shoes with fishnet stockings. I was angry at these girls and their perfect hairless bodies, but at the same time loved their beauty and craved their attention. Maybe I was just reacting to peer pressure since there was no chance I was ever going to be as bristle free as they were. There had already been one occasion at recess when my friends compared my ropey, brunette leg hair to their almost nonexistent hair. The thing is, peer pressure is called pressure because it will squeeze you into conformity until your eyeballs pop out and all good sense vanishes.

I was invited to Sarah Langley's twelfth birthday tea party, and all the girls had agreed to wear short summer dresses. I begged my mom to take me shopping for a sleeveless summer dress, and much to my surprise, she was happy that I was taking what she saw as the first step toward embracing my womanhood—which for her was about my femininity and for me was about my popularity.

We left for our shopping trip Saturday morning, the day of the party. After many stores, there it was at J.C. Penney: a Navy blue dress with a red and white polka dot cotton ruffle around the bottom. Sleeveless. White—oh-baby—fishnets with sandals completed the ensemble. We bought Sarah a gift and rushed home to primp for the afternoon party, now only an hour away. Before getting in the shower, I begged my mother to let me shave my legs. "*All* the girls are doing it, and they don't even *need* to! I have a black forest! It will be humiliating!"

"Your legs will be covered. Don't be silly. Your friends won't even notice."

"They will notice! Girls notice everything!"

She tried to appease me by promising to put a bun in my hair—quite the current rage. I grudgingly agreed and prayed everyone would not look below my cute bun and my sleek, new dress.

It came time to slip my God Bless America red, white, and blue creation over my head, and I lifted my arms in front of the vanity mirror in my bedroom. The dress settled over my new, slightly padded bra and my eyes met the mirror, arms still in the air, as I allowed the dress to slink into place. I watched my expectant eyeballs go from hope to horror. Oh God no! Growing in both scary armpits, like twin tarantulas, were repulsive shocks of dark, tangled, longer-than-life hair. I clamped my arms to my sides where I vowed they'd stay for the rest of my life.

With only twenty minutes until party time, I pulled my mother into the bathroom, shut the door, and lifted my arms. I saw the "Lord have mercy" look in her eyes before she realized that she could not in good conscience deny my request. "You can't let me go like this mom! Nobody else has trees growing under their arms like I do." My mother tried to resist, but only briefly. My pleading eyes, matched with the horrendous site of my pits, convinced her it was time. I slipped off the dress and, with a combination of scissors and my mother's razor, we landscaped my pits.

When my armpits were slick and shiny, as smooth as a baby's bottom, we slipped the dress back in place. With my leg hairs blowing in the breeze between each triangle of my white fish-net stockings, I was off to the party. I don't remember much about the party itself. I guess the pressure I felt in getting ready to see my friends was far more intense than the actual event.

My mother ended up letting me shave my legs the summer before seventh grade, and I was able to leave my body hair issues behind and go back to worrying about hairstyles. I tried all the styles that were in. It was the late sixties and there were shoulder-length flips to consider—should I flip my hair up or under like a cresting wave? There were parts and bangs to consider—should I part my hair on the side and let my bangs grow out, in the middle and keep my bangs, or some combination thereof? Many of my friends cut their hair short and ratted it high on top, with small sideburn curls around the face.

By high school, it was the early '70s and long, straight hippie hair was in. I parted it in the middle, grew out my bangs, and let my thick, shiny auburn hair trail down my back and past my waist. Simplest style ever. As a freshman and sophomore, I went to lots of football games that called for casual jeans and T-shirts with my long, straight hair blowing in the evening breeze. No sweat. I didn't go to dances during those years, so I didn't experience the pressure of deciding on a special hairdo for a big event. But when my first boyfriend and my first high school dance came along, it was not pretty.

I was a junior. I didn't think straight hair would be appropriate for my boyfriend's senior prom. I browsed through *Seventeen Magazine* and *Simplicity* sewing patterns for the perfect look and the perfect dress. I made a pink velvet, very short dress with ruching (a popular gathering stitch at the time) across the chest and elbow-length puff sleeves. I thought it was gorgeous. I curled my hair—which of course I never did anymore—flipping the ends and ratting it up in the right places. I wore makeup and eye shadow and extra layers of mascara. I sat in front of the large vanity mirror in the room I shared with my sister and saw the reflection of a completely overwhelmed sixteen-year-old face looking out from black eyes, a pile of ratted hair, and a frenzy of flouncy pink velvet. I started to cry, and it was all I could do not to rip off my dress, wash the makeup off my face, brush my hair out, put on my pjs, and crawl into bed. My mother came to the rescue moments before my date arrived, and used her magic fingers—that I had forgotten were magic—to adjust my makeup and hair in just the right ways. By the next day, I would forget again how much she could have influenced my future poor decisions if only I would have asked for her help.

Did You Know / Fun Facts

Hair Styles From My Mama's Time to Your Time

1940s First aerosol hairspray created. Shoulder-length, smooth, sculpted waves, curled at the bottom; "Victoria Rolls" pinned into buns at both temples.

1950s Short, layered cuts with curls and side-swept bangs (Marilyn Monroe) or long hair with short fringe (bangs).

1960s Styles in the '60s went from the beehive to long and flowing to free-spirited and natural (Janis Joplin) to short, short pixie styles (Twiggy).

1970s More natural looks like long straight hair (Ali McGraw), afros, or feathered hair (Farrah Fawcett).

1980s Hair was permed, sprayed, scrunched, or crimped with mousse, curling irons, or scrunchies into Big Hair.

1990s Flat iron introduced. Layered, bouncy shags in different lengths; "The Rachel" (Jennifer Aniston); box braids (Janet Jackson).

2000s Anything goes: perms, curls, bobs, straight, colors, braids, buns, buzz, bald.

Your Story

I returned to the high school where I taught for sixteen years to meet with students during the writing of this book. Rosalie, a freshman with long, thick, black hair had a hair story for me. When she was about to begin middle school, she wanted a new look to go with her new school and new maturity. She asked her mother if she could cut her hair as her gift for graduating from elementary school. She told me, "My mom was strict with hair. She grew up in Ixmiquilpan, Hidalgo, Mexico, and my father was from Oaxaca, Mexico. The tradition was for women to have long hair, which they braided." The conversation with her mom went something like this:

"Mom, I want a new hair style as a graduation gift. I want to cut my hair."

"How much do you want to cut off?"

"I want to leave my hair long on one side and shave one side from the part down."

"No, you will look like a boy."

"I'll just shave a small section."

"You can shave from your hair part down to your ear, but only two inches wide."

Rosalie continued, "When I got to the hair stylist, I asked my mom if I could have a star design cut into the shaved side. The hair stylist thought it was a good idea and tried to talk her into it, but my mom refused."

I asked her how it went afterwards when friends and family saw her with the new style. "I learned a lot from the reactions of other people. My cousin was a senior in high school, and he said, 'Why are you trying to be black? You look like a boy now.' My feelings were hurt because I expected them to say, 'Oh, that's a new look. It looks nice.' I tried not to show that my feelings were hurt and just rolled my eyes and said sarcastically, 'Oh, you're funny.'"

Rosalie shared that her uncle thought of himself as a father figure to her. When he saw her, he said, "You shouldn't have done that. You look like a boy." When her mom heard other people's reactions to the cut, she said, "I kind of regret letting you do it." She explained that when she was growing up, her family was very poor. Sometimes they would get lice, and her parents would shave their hair off completely. Shaving any part of her hair was a negative, embarrassing experience.

When Rosalie was fifteen, she bleached her black hair, then grew it out again, then cut it off, and when she was seventeen, she tried bangs for the first time. "Sometimes I regret cutting my hair back then. Maybe I shouldn't have done it, but hair always grows back."

Maya, Rosalie's friend, also wanted to talk about her long, curly hair. She told me that when she was young, she felt frustrated when her hair frizzed, especially in the front. She began cutting off the frizz where she could see it around her face until she ended up with sort of a fringe look in the front. One day, she and her mom were going to the grocery store, and her mom noticed that something was different.

"What the heck happened to your hair?"

"Nothing. I cut it."

"Are you dumb? Why would you cut your hair?"

Her mother forgot about the trip to the grocery store and stopped in front of a barbershop. She made Maya get out of the car and said, "This is what happens when you try to trim your own hair!"

"No, no! Please don't make me cut my hair!"

"Pushing me through the door, my mother said to the barber, 'Cut off her hair. She's made a mess of it.'"

Maya told me, "It was right before I was entering middle school, and I was so embarrassed by my short hair. To this day, my hair has never grown as long as it was then." Looking back on it, Maya says, "I would rather have had a whooping than have my hair cut. When my mom and I talk about it now, we both hold to our stories. My mom thinks she was right, and I think she shouldn't have made me cut my hair. The difference is, now I get that what I did was wrong."

What I Wish My Mama Would Have Told Me

I wish my mama would have told me that every woman has the right to decide what she wants to do with the hair on her body. I wish she would have said, "You can have hair under your armpits *à la* French women if you want to. You can shave the hair on your legs and choose fishnets or dresses or short shorts if you want to. Or you can have hair on your legs and let it fly. If you want to shave, by all means, go ahead and shave. But you have a choice." I wish she would have asked me, "Why, my sweet daughter, do you want to shave your legs? If it is to impress your girlfriends or to fit in or to catch your first boyfriend, it's still okay. Just be aware that is your motive, and consider whether that motive deserves your attention."

I wish my mama would have told me that pressure from my peers didn't have to influence all of my decisions. I wish she would have told me that it's okay to make very personal, one-of-a-kind decisions about hair, makeup, clothes, and the friends with whom I felt most comfortable. I wish she would have told me that I didn't need to hang out with people who questioned—and made me question—whether I was smart enough, good enough, strong enough to make decisions that were best for me. I wish she would have told me that when I felt all the pressures—from my friends, boyfriend, and even myself—she would be there for me.

Opportunities to Journal

* Describe a time you felt pressured by someone to wear your hair a certain way, dress a certain way, or act a certain way. How did this make you feel?

* If you can't think of a time, describe a time you've seen this happen to someone else.

* Is it possible to be yourself in the face of all the peer pressure? What can help you have courage?

* Have you ever made a decision that went against what most people were doing? How did it feel?

Take-Aways

* Hair is an important part of your individual look. It can cause you anxiety and pressure, and can affect how you feel about your body image.

✻ Pressure from your peers and your parents can affect decisions you make about how you look.

✻ It's important to choose your own look and style, perhaps to respectfully defend your choices. Sometimes, when you dress and choose hairstyles that are popular, you end up being uncomfortable in your own skin . . . and hair.

✻ Sometimes you may feel scared and vulnerable as a result of these pressures and will need to communicate your needs to parents or someone else you trust.

✻ You may not learn until later *why* you wanted to try a new style, and you may even regret the decision. The more time you take making the right decision for *you*, the better chance you'll have of being comfortable with who you are.

Chapter 3

Friendship & Bullying

You know those times when you feel like you're on the outside of your group of friends looking in? You're listening to what's being said, but no one is really acknowledging you? Maybe you've even walked up to your friends and overheard them talking in a snarky way about a mutual friend who isn't there. Do you wonder if they ever talk about you like that? Or maybe you've had a friend comment critically on social media about a new outfit you wore or a new hairstyle you tried. Did you ask yourself, "Is she serious? How am I supposed to take that?"

Let's take a look at how the word *friend* has changed since social media platforms were introduced. A traditional definition for *friend* includes phrases like "attached to another by affection," or "one that is not hostile," or "a favored companion who shows kindly interest and goodwill." Social media, on the other hand, has redefined the word *friend* to simply mean someone added to your social media site. Sometimes we don't even actually know a *friend* because it's a celebrity account or friend of a friend. We accept friends and look for their "likes" or "loves" to gain approval.

It can be confusing because someone who is labeled a friend can be the same person who criticized that new outfit yesterday. Have you ever wondered when those comments cross the line and become bullying? Maybe you've even posted a negative or angry comment that you wish you could take back. Does that make you a bully?

We can fight against being a bully by treating everyone with respect. We can be supportive friends. Sometimes the truest friend comes from a moment when we reach out and become a friend to someone else. We can fight against being bullied by carrying ourselves with pride, standing tall, holding our heads high, and walking with purpose. And sometimes we will realize a friend was never really a friend at all. Some friends may come into our lives to teach us lessons about ourselves that makes us stronger in the end. Friends do not define us, but when we feel rejected, we can seek help from an adult we trust (see **Resources**).

My Story

When I went to middle school, I felt abandoned by many of my friends. We had been in orchestra together in elementary school, but some decided it wouldn't be cool to continue. They found new friends. No one ever talked about "bullying," and my old friends never said anything mean to my face; they just ignored me when they passed me in the halls. I do remember the feelings of rejection. I found three new girlfriends that shared orchestra with me, and we bonded and became a posse of four.

By the time I was in high school, I had a new set of friends who shared classes and extracurricular activities with me. I remained in the orchestra, but only one of my middle school group of three came to the same high school with me. She and I remained friends throughout high school. I hung out with some great students whom I met in English, World History, Spanish, and gym class my freshman year, and out of those students only one became a life-long friend.

Even with my new friends, I longed to be acknowledged by my old friends who were part of my earliest memories. In high school, thinking we would all be more mature now, I said "Hi" in the halls, but there was still no answer. One particular friend from the past bothered me the most. We'll call her Judy. She was tall and slender with large, round blue eyes and short blonde hair. In all honesty, Judy probably prepared me the most for what girls can be like in middle school, high school, and for the rest of my life. In elementary school, I spent a lot of time in Judy's home, and she in mine, before appearances mattered so much. I loved her sisters and her mother. For some reason, her rejection of me hurt more than some of the other girls. When I returned to my high school reunion ten years after graduating, I was looking forward to the cliques of high school being dissolved so that we could all love one another again. I saw Judy across the room, surrounded by a group of people. I walked up to her and said, "Judy! Hi! How are you! It's so great to see you!" She was looking away, smiling at someone across the room, and had to turn towards my voice. When she saw it was me, the "I'm so popular" smile left her face and she said, "Oh. Hello," and turned her back to me, continuing as if I wasn't even there. I was twenty-eight years old, divorced, remarried, the mother of three children, and she took me right back to middle school in a short second.

As I thought about Judy and other friends that had been so special to me when I was a younger student, I decided to pull out my high school yearbooks and look some of them up. First of all, I was shocked to find that many names and stories scribbled in the front and back pages of my yearbook I couldn't remember at all. Second of all, when I looked up the names of my elementary school friends in the index, I was equally shocked to find out that about fifteen—out of those names I could remember—went to my high school. Did I know that back in the '70s? Why didn't I have contact with them in high school? Six of them I had been very close to, and two of those six were girls who had stopped being my friends. Two of them were from the same church I went to. Three were neighbors. I began to wonder if I had ignored them the same way I had been ignored by elementary and middle school friends. It was an unsettling feeling.

I found out later that bullying can be emotional, verbal, or physical; it can be subtle or obvious. Maybe I had ignored or rejected some of my old friends the same way I felt rejected. Maybe, in a way, I had been a bully without realizing it. I did some research about bullying in the '70s to help me figure out why I didn't specifically remember bullying incidents from high school. In the '70s, people didn't label or talk about bullying, abuse, eating disorders, stress, or suicide (see **Chapter 6**). When I was in high school, what is now thought of as bullying was simply viewed as part of growing up. We heard sayings like, "Sticks and stones will break your bones, but words will never hurt you," and "Kids will be kids." There was no mention of the word "bullying" in any school policies before the 1980s when bullying began to be depicted in popular movies as a form of entertainment.

When I looked through my yearbook pictures, a few memories were triggered. There was the girl with the buckteeth and the girl who had a small third breast with a nipple growing off to the side, kind of under one arm. (We knew because of those gym class showers.) There was the boy who was more effeminate than most and the guy who had terrible dandruff that could be seen through his hair and all over his clothes. There was the painfully shy girl whose mother was an alcoholic. It was easier for her not to have friends so that she would never have to invite anyone to her home. I only knew about her because she was a neighbor, and I was one of the very few who saw what it was like behind her front door. There was the girl with mild Down syndrome who had a very large head, large eyes, and had to think extra long before responding. I know there was giggling and quiet talking behind their backs; I witnessed it. I didn't witness—although it may have happened—anything said directly to these people.

In looking at homecoming pictures my senior year, I was reminded of a bullying scheme that backfired on the bullies, much to the joy of most of the student body. There was a funny, super smart, stocky, athletic girl who I'll call Nadine. As a joke, she was nominated by the football players to be homecoming queen. She knew why they had done it, but instead of being hurt, she embraced it and kept her name on the ballot. All of us who knew her—in her AP classes, in the clubs she was a member of, in her sports teams, and eventually those who hadn't known her before, but heard what was going on—voted for her. She ended up being in the top ten girls. She dressed beautifully on homecoming night, one of five escorts to the girls who were the front-runners. I think this was an attempt to bully before the term "bullying" was used, and fortunately friends had her back and didn't let it happen.

It has taken me years to realize that friends come in and out of our lives to teach us lessons that we need to learn at the time. Sometimes the friendships make us stronger or make us realize what kind of person we want to be. Sometimes the friendships teach us about compassion and culture and acceptance. Bullying, whether named or not, is hurtful and painful, and has lasting effects. What I have found is that the common denominator in being able to survive and heal from bullying is the same: friendship. Whether the friend is an old friend, new friend, or a hardly-known friend, when we stick up for each other and speak out against abuse of any kind, we are stronger. In high school, I could have easily reached out to the past friends who didn't reject me. Maybe, just like me, they were feeling ignored and left out.

Did You Know? / Not-So-Fun Facts

Bullying

Tip for looking at the bullying chart: Look through the possible characteristics of the bully or the bullied and see whether, like me, you can find yourself in some way in either or both lists rather than viewing them from the outside.

Bullying consists of three basic types of abuse: emotional, verbal and physical. It can be subtle or obvious.

Cyber bulling consists of harassing, humiliating, intimidating, or threatening others on the internet. It includes sending cruel, vicious or threatening messages; creating websites that have stories, cartoons, pictures, or jokes ridiculing others; posting pictures of classmates online and asking students to rate them on derogatory features; engaging someone in instant messaging with threatening or derogatory comments (see **Chapter 4**).

Possible Characteristics of Bullies

Someone who . . .

- has a big ego, may be violent and has no empathy for his/her targets.

- uses rumors, gossip and verbal taunts. Isolates targets and excludes his/her targets from social activities.

- is cool and detached. Can be vicious and vindictive towards target, but can be charming in front of others. Bullies when no one is looking.

- does not process social cues correctly. May react aggressively, believing others are out to get him/her.

- in a group, behaves in ways he/she wouldn't if alone.

- comes together in a gang to have power or control over others. The gang may see that they are part of a family and have a territory to protect. They usually do not show empathy or remorse.

Possible Characteristics of the Bullied

Someone who . . .

- is new to the neighborhood or school (may be the youngest, smallest, most insecure).

- has been previously traumatized and finds it hard to ask for help.

- is submissive, anxious, lacking in self-confidence and tries to please or placate others.

- has behaviors others find annoying.

- is unwilling to fight and prefers to resolve conflicts without aggression.

- is shy, reserved, quiet, unassuming, timid, sensitive, or expresses emotions readily.

- is poor or rich.

- has a race, ethnicity, or religion that is viewed by the bully as inferior.

- stands out because he's different. May be bright, talented, gifted, or have a physical or mental disability.

- is independent and unconcerned about social status, doesn't conform to the norm.

- is fat, thin, short, tall, wears braces or glasses, has acne or other skin conditions.

What to Do to Help End Bullying

- Treat everyone with respect.

- Stop and think before you say or do something that could hurt someone. Everyone is different. Not better or worse—just different.

- Be a friend to the person being bullied. Include them by sitting with them at lunch or on the bus, talking to them at school, hanging out with them to show them they are not alone.

- Stand up for the person being bullied and/or report the bullying to an adult you trust.

- Whether you are the bully or the person being bullied, seek help from an adult you trust. Not saying anything makes it worse for everyone.

What to Do if You Are Being Bullied

- Look at the person bullying you and tell him or her to stop in a calm, clear voice.

- If speaking up seems too hard or not safe, walk away and stay away.

- Don't fight back.

- Find an adult to stop the bullying on the spot.

- Talk to an adult you trust and make a plan to stop the bullying.

- Stay away from places where bullying happens.

- Stay near adults and other kids. Most bullying happens when adults aren't around.

- Call 911 or a bullying support line (see **Resources**).

Your Story

Today, schools are required to have policies regarding bullying. Bullying must be defined and addressed in school codes. Unfortunately, the ability for students to bully—especially verbal and emotional abuse—has increased because of computers, cell phones, digital cameras, and other technological devices. Cyber bullying was added to state laws and school codes in 2008.

Ana, a sophomore I interviewed at a local high school, shared with me a bullying incident that happened to her friend on Facebook:

"We have a group of friends that talk all the time on Facebook. There is a guy named Joe, his best friend, Pam, Amy, and me. One day Pam shared on Facebook, 'Tag if you would wear these.' She put a meme of a picture of cutesy painted jeans on a little girl. She tagged a girl we all know who wears a pair of jeans that looks like they have paint all over them, but it's just the style; she bought them that way. Someone else posted, 'LMAO (laughing my ass off). When you can't afford jeans so you have to buy them at a thrift store.' Lots of people were liking her comment."

Ana told me she got upset at Pam, who shared the meme, and others who were liking the comments, so she posted, "You have no right to make fun of her because you don't know the situation." Another friend commented to Pam, "How are you talking? You wear the same jeans every day." Ana admitted that cyber bullying is a negative consequence of social media and being online all the time. She said, "The internet makes us vulnerable. It's a dangerous place and we can become addicted to it. Our social skills go down."

Josie, a high school junior, tried to hold onto her best friend of three years, Monica, until she began to feel bullied by her. She explained that, "After middle school, we went to different high schools, and she began to change. She wasn't the same person I became friends with. She hung around people that weren't good for her, and eventually got kicked out of her home." Even though Josie and her friend didn't see each other as much, Josie felt that she always listened and supported her.

She said, "I rarely got myself into trouble. It wasn't like me to act out. But this one night I was hanging out with my boyfriend and ended up sleeping over because it was late. I told my sister, but I guess she never told my mom."

Josie's mother called Monica and other friends to see if they knew where she was, and worried all night about where she might be.

"Monica was worried too, but ended up getting mad and ignoring me instead of trying to understand what happened. I tried telling her that everything was a misunderstanding, but she kept ignoring me."

Josie told me that she felt bullied as a result of Monica spreading rumors about her. "She said I left my best friend for my boyfriend and called me a 'fake bitch.'"

Because rumors travel so much faster with the help of cell phones and social media, by the end of the day, Josie felt that everybody was viewing her as this person Monica had portrayed.

"I needed someone to sit and listen and be there for me, but instead I was not taken seriously and blamed for what happened to our friendship. It made me feel that I could not trust and depend on others, and this is why I don't really have friends now."

Another girl named Asia shared that she often feels bullied by her classmates, but also by her family. She says that she lost some of her self-confidence when she had to move to San Diego, away from her childhood friends.

"That's when I started eating more than I usually would. I didn't really notice that I was gaining weight until I started getting bullied by my peers and my family members. I was already stressed as a kid because I had been bullied as a result of my dark skin. Endless nights I would cry to myself, asking why I wasn't skinny like everyone else in my class. My mom didn't pay any attention to the bullying because 'who would listen to a kid?'"

Asia shared a little bit about how she began to feel better about herself. "As a kid, you're supposed to have a good childhood and have fun, but it wasn't like that for me. I really never had friends, and people would avoid talking to me or they would talk about me; that made me even more stressed."

Her advice? "If you have trouble loving yourself, see what the problem is and try to fix it. For example, I eventually lost weight and set goals for myself to make sure I wasn't giving up on myself. Loving yourself isn't going to be easy at first, and it takes time. It takes steps, but you are going to get there."

What I Wish My Mama Would Have Told Me

I wish my mama would have told me that friends come and go in your life, and in the end you will have one best friend from middle school and one best friend from high school with whom you will have a life-time connection . . . if you're lucky.

I wish my mama would have helped me evaluate my friendships, learn lessons from the ones that went by the wayside, and hold on tightly to the ones that show signs of lasting forever. I wish my mama would have told me that the tenuous relationships teach us lessons and the significant relationships remain to bolster us through the difficult times and give us companionship and joy in the good times. The tenuous relationships were not about our self-worth; they were to help us recognize ourselves in all of our complexity and lead us to recognize the powerful young women we would become.

I wish my mama would have told me, "Have friends, but don't rely on friends to make you who you are. Your self-esteem is not connected to the whims of childhood friends. If you want to enjoy friendship more, be a friend; don't just have a friend. There are probably many girls and boys in your class who feel rejected by you because you are part of this elite clique of popular girls. What would happen if you would be a friend to them instead of worrying so much about who wants to be friends with you?"

I wish she would have told me that sometimes I would feel so low after a friend's rejection that I might even want to take my life (see **Chapter 6**). Being rejected by a girlfriend or boyfriend hurts. I wish she would have told me that whatever I'm feeling is important. "These feelings you are having when your friendships don't go as planned are not to be taken lightly. You are not alone."

Opportunities to Journal

* Have you had any friends who used to be best friends, but aren't in your life any more? What happened? How did it make you feel?
* Has anyone said anything unkind or unfair to you or about you in a text, email, or on social media? What happened? How did you feel about the incident?
* Have you ever witnessed someone being bullied? What did you do? Do you wish you would have responded differently?

Take-Aways

* In the dictionary, "friend" is defined by phrases like "attached by affection" or showing "kindly interest and good will." Social media, on the other hand, has redefined "friend" to simply mean someone added to your social media site.
* Bullying of any kind is never okay. Treating everyone with respect and including everyone is important. Being a supportive friend can help both bullies and those being bullied.
* Carry yourself with pride. Stand tall, hold your head up high, and walk with purpose. Your body posture sends a message, "Don't mess with me. I'm confident."
* Whether a friend is an old friend, new friend, or a hardly-known friend, when we stick up for each other and speak out against

abuse of any kind, we are stronger.

✱ Cyber bullying is a negative consequence of social media. The ability for students to bully—especially verbal and emotional abuse—has increased because of computers, cell phones, digital cameras, and other technological devices.

✱ Being rejected or bullied by someone hurts. Losing a friendship because of bullying or being bullied can hurt to the point of wanting to take your life. Seek help from an adult you trust (see **Resources**).

Chapter 4

Social Media

Do you ever find that you sit down to check your email or social media accounts and, before you know it, you've been sitting in front of the screen for an hour or more? Have you mindlessly scrolled through the latest app or website instead of doing homework? Do you ever end up seeing comments, events, or just random information that you wish you didn't know? Do you ever feel just a little depressed, overwhelmed, or stressed out when you are done?

The bad news is that sometimes when we engage in social media, we feel pressure to look good, go to cool places, show our best selves, or be in a relationship. We feel stress worrying about likes and dislikes, friends who went to a movie without us, or a bullying comment posted by a "friend." We can even become addicted to clicking in the "feedback loop," posting selfies and comments, reading comments, counting "likes" and "dislikes."

The good news is that we have the power to make decisions about social media that keep us healthier and happier. We can keep in contact with friends and family, organize events, follow current news, fashion, makeup, and social trends. We can meet friends for conversations and video games. We can monitor our own technology use and pay attention to how we feel when we are engaged with social media. We can express our creative selves.

My Story

When I was in high school, there was no internet. We followed trends primarily through popular teen magazines. *Seventeen Magazine* was first published in 1944, and was geared to thirteen- to nineteen-year-old females. Its purpose then was to inspire teen girls to become model workers and citizens. It was the first magazine ever that specifically targeted teens.

In the 1970s, when I was in high school, the magazine was full of fashion articles like "5 Top Teen Models Tell How They Start Their Day Right," "Fashion Festival: New Looks for Early Birds," "4 Makeover Dreams Come True," and "Beauty: Are You Wearing Last Year's Face?" It also helped me decide how to attract my first boyfriend: "New Color Clues to Your Personality," "Calorie-Saving Coolers," and "What to Wear, How to Look to Add to the Scenery." Once I got the boy, I could learn more about him with "What a Boy's Handwriting Tells You."

More importantly, but apparently often ignored by sixteen-year-old me, controversial subjects were also included, like the draft, race, homosexuality, the environment, sex, and drugs. Although I don't remember this explicitly, history tells me that in the summer of my fifteenth year, when I was swimming at the local pool, being kissed by an older man after tennis matches and wondering if I was too fat for my first two-piece bathing suit, the first black woman ever to appear on a fashion magazine cover happened in the July 1971 issue of *Seventeen*. Later when I was a junior dating my first boyfriend, cover stories included "The Dating Scene around the World," "Answers to Your Most-Asked Questions on Birth Control," "When You're Single and Pregnant," and "Abortion: The Toughest Decision of All." That particular issue was just months before the *Roe v. Wade* Supreme Court decision.

If I had been paying attention, I would have been learning that women and women's issues were becoming more and more important in the world at large. Women were beginning to have a voice. Even though at home I was receiving messages about how to be a beautiful wife who cooks and cleans and takes care of the family, the new messages about individual strength and opportunities for women were being written—within the *Seventeen Magazine* sitting on our coffee table. At the time, I didn't realize the difficult, conflicting messages I was getting that I could take advantage of these opportunities, but not at the expense of my responsibilities as a girlfriend, wife, and future mother.

I was a teenager after all, and I was engaged in the—more important to me—issues of fashion, makeup, and surveys about boyfriends. I regret that. You'll find out why soon.

Did You Know/Not-So-Fun Facts

Social Media

Many studies have been conducted to find out how social media is affecting children, teens, and adults. These are some of the facts and observations I found:

- A UK study of 14- to 24-year-olds found that social media led to increased feelings of depression, anxiety, poor body image and loneliness.

- A two-year comparison showed 25% of teens had smart phones in 2012 and by 2014 75% of teens had smart phones.

- According to a Pew study of 13- to 17-year-olds, screen time among teens is increasing. In 2014–15, 24% of teens said they are online "almost constantly." In 2018, 45% of teens said the same thing.

- Most teens are online or onscreen 6.5–9 hours a day.

- Ivy League Colleges are now checking potential students' social media accounts to make sure they are getting well-rounded students. Harvard recently rescinded admission offers to ten students who shared offensive images in a Facebook chat room. The students thought the chat room was private.

- Teens may feel partly anonymous when they're on social media or online. As a result, they make choices they would not make in face-to-face situations.

- Social media magnifies everything that happens to teens. In real life, three or four people might see something happen; online, that number can increase quickly until mob mentality goes into effect, and reactions can become mean-spirited.

- Marketing companies and influencers (famous or more casual teen vloggers who talk about a product) use teens' accessible information to target them as consumers. Sex traffickers may present themselves as teen boys to target teen girls as products.

- In the 2000s social media can negatively influence teens because of factors like:

    1) Persistence (all information sticks around longer);

    2) Editing/modifying (we can't control what others do to our pictures or information);

    3) Sharing (information can be instantly shared to hundreds of people);

    4) Searching (it is easy for anyone to find out your information).

What Teens Can Do (from interviews with teens):

- Don't put too many selfies on your social media pages.

- Don't ever post naked or suggestive pictures. Don't act older than you are. You might think a cute boy is looking when the person is actually a creepy older man, or even worse. You could be putting yourself in danger.

- Delete mean comments or block people who leave them. The number of likes or dislikes you have does not determine your self-worth.

- Balance your time on the computer and social media. Set a timer or ask your parents for help.

- Figure out who you are without the help of social media. Are you really the same person that you show on your social media account? Or are you just projecting who you think you should be?

- Increase the time you talk to friends and family face to face.

- Choose to keep parts of your life private (privacy is when you are free from being observed or disturbed by other people).

- Be aware of how your phone and your social media accounts are making you feel. Positive? Less stressed? More stressed? Distracted from actual reality?

What Parents Can Do:

- Talk to teens about why excessive screen time can be unhealthy and be completely open about your desire to monitor online activity.

- Set a digital curfew and power the phone in a different room than the one the teen sleeps in.

- Use apps to monitor teens' use of their phones, social media and internet (like bark, Netsanity®, Net Nanny®, TeenSafe, and Limitly). Tell your teen that you are monitoring and tell them why.

- Steer teens to TED Talks by teenagers on many topics, including social media use.

- Have open discussions with your teen about bullying, sexting, predators, depression, anxiety and suicide.

- Research the ways that social media users hide accounts, like real Instagram accounts (rinsta accounts) vs. friends-only or fake accounts (finsta accounts). Find out how users hide apps in order to store photos and videos they don't want discovered.

Your Story

What I learned from teens today is that some things haven't changed all that much—like being more interested in looks, clothes, hair, friends, and the opposite sex than in politics and social justice; and some things have changed a lot—like how you get your information. A teen can read magazines today, including *Seventeen* and *Vogue*, and many others that tell her far more than could be published in the 1970s, but she is more likely to conduct internet searches and check out social media sites. It doesn't mean teens aren't interested in politics or social justice or any other topic affecting our world; it's just that there are so many other topics—just by the nature of being a teen—that might be more interesting.

A teen girl can put in a search phrase for a question she has about boys or sex and end up accidentally on a porn site. She can find out lots of information, true and not true, appropriate and not appropriate. It's often hard to decipher. She can be innocently posting on Facebook and end up scammed by a much older sex offender. Her messages can be misrepresented through editing or photoshopping from an outside source. She can fall in love through a dating site and end up kidnapped by a sex trafficking ring. She can see that teens all around her are becoming famous on YouTube and become obsessed with fame. She can become lost in the insanity of "I can be anything I want to be, and yet I can't keep up with YouTube teens or reality show teens."

No teenage girl starts out thinking that something she is doing or saying on social media is going to put her in danger. She doesn't think that by copying poses and styles from the ads in the latest *Seventeen Magazine* or a social media site, that she's sending messages to some unknown viewer on Facebook whom she cannot see. Some of those messages we've already talked about can still influence choices that seem fun and innocent:

"You've got to be sexy for guys. Shave those pits, legs, and pubes, and show him how smooth you are."

"Show those breasts off. If they're small, wear a push-up bra. In fact, wear the bra in your snapshot or just underneath a see-through tank top."

"Outline those beautiful eyes with dark, black eyeliner and lengthen those eyelashes you were born with by painting layer upon layer of mascara."

"You're only thirteen? That's okay. The guys searching the internet will never know."

Rarely in these high school dramas did a young girl wake up one day and want to be sexually exploited or taken advantage of in any way.

Here's what I found out from teens about social media

Positives:

* My Instagram account makes me more confident because I post pictures and people "like" them. I feel accepted and validated when I get a lot of likes or followers.

* I am able to keep in contact with family and friends that I don't get to see very often.

* I can keep current with news updates.

* I can follow people I admire and learn about fashion, makeup, and social trends.

* I have a place to support friends and stick up for them if they are being bullied.

* I can use my account to organize events and reach more people.

* I can go on video game sites and play with people I don't know. I make a lot of new friends.

* I can talk about topics that are hard for me to talk about face to face.

* I can express my talents and creativity. I can even become famous and rich.

Negatives:

* There's a lot of pressure to look good and have a great body. I have more expectations about what my body should look like because of social media and I compare myself to others.

* Sometimes I measure how much people like me and whether I'm a popular person by how many likes my pictures get. If I don't get likes, I feel criticized.

* Some posts are too personal; some of my friends over-share, and have too many selfies. It's hard to keep my life private because I'm expected to share even when I don't want to.

* I waste too much time on my social media accounts and don't get my homework done. I can get lost in it, and then I end up stressed and in trouble.

* Cyber-bullying is a real problem. It's happened to me, and it's happened to many of my friends. Some "friends" get revenge by posting mean comments that aren't true when they think they've been wronged.

* There is more pressure now to go to cool places because it looks like everyone else is having more fun. This affects my self-esteem in a negative way. I know that my own Instagram pictures don't mean that I have that life all the time, but it's hard to remember that when I see the cool pictures others post.

* I am not always in charge of how I am presented because others post pictures or comments about me too. Sometimes people judge me more and talk about my mistakes.

* There is also pressure to show the best version of myself because family, teachers, and even future colleges might be watching.

* There is pressure to be in a relationship and show pictures of a boyfriend or girlfriend. When the relationship ends, everybody knows about it.

* I get jealous when I see invitations to a party that I'm not invited to, or pictures where my friends went out together to dinner or a movie and I wasn't invited.

* Comments or pictures I didn't even want posted can be seen by all of my friends and family or even go viral. People can also photoshop my pictures and make it look like I was doing something I wasn't or wearing something I wasn't.

* It's easy to misunderstand comments and texts because I'm not face to face with the person, and I can't see their eyes or body language. It's hard to know what they really mean. I've gotten my feelings hurt, and I've hurt friends before.

I wanted to confirm the research, so I spent some good face-to-face time with a few teens at Hoover High School. Rhonda told me a story about how high school relationships, especially break-ups, can blow up on social media. And not only because of friends—also because of parents. Her friend, Gabriela, had been going out with a guy for about a year—we'll call him Alex. She broke up with him because he cheated on her. In this case, "cheated" meant going out with another girl and making out with her. He told the girl he went out with that he wasn't in a relationship.

Rhonda told me the story:

The girl messaged Gabriela on Facebook and said, "I went out with your boyfriend. I thought he was single, but I checked his Facebook and saw he had a girlfriend. Are you Alex's girlfriend?" Gabriela said yes, and the girl sent a screenshot of a text conversation between Alex and her. She told Gabriela, "Go ask him; he's lying to you. I want you to know because I've been cheated on before and I know how it feels."

Gabriela confronted Alex by text, and he denied it. She said to him, "Why are you denying when I know the truth?" They had a big argument.

Then Gabriela's mother got involved and messaged Alex's account. She wrote, "Why would you do this to my daughter? We trusted you. You treat her like she's a piece of crap. You're an asshole."

Friends got involved too and supported Gabriela, calling Alex a cheater and posting other negative comments about him. Rhonda, Gabriela, and another girlfriend went into a chat room, and Gabriela told the girls, "Stop insulting him. Ignore him. It is what it is."

I had lots of questions about regular Facebook posts versus messaging versus chat rooms. I asked Rhonda if it was common for parents to get involved in the conversations. She said that it doesn't always happen, but sometimes it does. She said, "I don't think parents should get involved. It just makes the situation worse. Gabriela was right to ask people to stop making comments at all."

Sara, a sophomore cheerleader, agreed that too many relationship details, especially break-ups, are aired on social media. She said that when she and her boyfriend broke up, she unfriended him on Instagram because it was hard emotionally for her to see what he was doing and who he was hanging out with.

She said, "When I unfriended him, he started saying ugly things about me on his Instagram account. He didn't go to the same high school as me, so I would get information from other people we were both friends with."

Next, friends began to take sides. Her best friend—who happened to be a guy—was angry about what Sara's ex was saying. He asked Sara if she wanted him to talk to the ex and tell him to stop making comments about Sara. On the day I talked to Sara, she had not decided whether she was going to have him talk to her ex or not. We talked about whether she could set and communicate the boundary herself, and what that might sound or look like (see **Chapter 22** on Boundaries).

What I Wish My Mama Would Have Told Me

I wish my mama would have told me that just because I am a girl, I am not an object to be branded or advertised. I can choose who I want to be and how I want to be seen by others. I wish she would have told me that no girl or boy in my life needs to know everything about me. No trend that ever shows its face in any magazine (or now social media) needs to be followed by me unless I want to follow it. It's okay to want and need and have privacy. I wish she would have said, "If you do follow the latest trend, simply ask yourself, why? If you clearly understand that the trend, whether mainstream or underground, is just a trend—that your individuality doesn't have anything to do with the color of your hair, the shape of your body, or the clothes you wear—then by all means do it."

If I were a teen of the 2000s, I think I would want to know that likes, loves, comments, and followers do not indicate how popular I am. I would want my mama to caution me not to get caught up in the feedback loop, posting and sharing images and videos I believe will get me the most reaction. I would want my mama to tell me, "Your values may become confused in the world of instantaneous feedback. Your online values may be based on how others are responding to your posts, rather than your real-life values given to you by family."

Opportunities to Journal

* What messages do you get about who/what you should be when you read your favorite magazine, blog, social media, or website?
* What kind of pressure do you feel from social media about how you should look/feel or what you should become?
* Do you know anyone who had a relationship on Facebook that turned out to be a scam? If so, what happened?
* What are your concerns about using social media and the way it makes you feel?

Take-Aways

* The bad news: Social media and internet use has negatives like pressure to look good, go to cool places, show your best self, and be in a relationship. Cyber-bullying, worrying about likes and dislikes, spending too much time in accounts, and jealousy over friends and events can cause depression and anxiety.
* The good news: We have the power to make decisions about social media that keep us healthier and happier. We can keep in

contact with friends and family, organize events, keep current with news, fashion, makeup and social trends, and meet friends for conversations and video games. We can monitor our own technology use and pay attention to how we feel when we are engaged with social media. We can express our creative selves.

* There is some risk attached to social media. Innocent searches can land you on a porn site or make you susceptible to scams from predators. Your messages can be misrepresented through editing or photoshopping from an outside source. Facebook pictures and poses can make you vulnerable to sex offenders or even sex trafficking rings.

* It's okay to choose for yourself what trends you want to follow, how much privacy you want and need, and how important the social media feedback loop is to you. You can decide whether you want to pay more attention to your real-life values than to your social media values.

Chapter 5

Gender Roles Then & Now

What messages do you get from family, social media, television, or movies about what is appropriate for a girl to do and be? Have you ever gotten the message that girls should have different hobbies, goals, occupations, or futures than boys? Have you ever been told to dress a certain way or wear your hair a certain way because you're a girl? Have you been asked to do inside jobs like cooking and cleaning while your brother does outside jobs like mowing the lawn and putting oil in the car?

Thankfully, our roles as women in society are changing and becoming more powerful and creative than they were for my mother and for me. Gender roles are about our abilities, passions, education, and dreams for the future. Expectations for the roles of men and women in society have changed and are continuing to change. We are all called on to take an active part in continuing to create change around sexual roles. We can choose any job we are qualified for, whether or not that job has traditionally been held by men.

The sex with which we are born is only biological. It refers to the body parts we had at birth. Most people are born male or female, but some people are born with anatomy or genetics that do not correspond to the typical expectations for either sex (see **Chapter 11**). Gender is more complex and has to do with how we express our traits and the characteristics that are normally attributed to men or women by society. Gender roles are always changing based on the cultural norms around us.

My Story

I was one of four girls, but when it came my turn to be a mother, I had boys. Three boys. I had no boy skills, but I knew that I didn't want my sons to learn all of their lessons during gym class from macho guys who pretended they'd had multiple sexual encounters by the time they were sixteen. I wanted them to learn about sex, but I also wanted them to learn about how to be funny, honest, hard-working, fair, respectful young men who would make solid partners for the person they would one day choose, if they chose to have a partner at all.

I enrolled them in courses called "Sex and the Whole Person." The classes were sponsored by our church, but were not religious in content. They took one course in middle school and another when they were in high school. The point of the two courses was a little different for each age group, but the important bottom lines were that 1) sex isn't dirty or secret, and 2) in order to understand sex, we must understand sexuality. Sexuality is more about the roles of boys and girls and men and women in society. They learned that society has different expectations for men than for women. They explored stereotypes about those roles and learned ways that they could fight against them in their own relationships. Ultimately, they would be armed with information about societal expectations of men and women—some of which are ridiculous and unfair—so that they could stand up for themselves and fight for equality between the sexes.

They had fun brainstorming every word they'd ever heard for penis, vagina, breasts, masturbation, having sex. Who talks about this stuff? It was hilarious. I got to be a counselor and participate in some of the shenanigans. They got to look at over fifty pictures of naked people and compare the difference between *National Geographic*-naked and *Playboy*-naked. They wrote down their emotions and reactions based on how a naked person was photographed. They got to have conversations and debate whether these naked people were being exploited or not. They had a blast playing the roles of husband or wife and recognizing whether they held stereotypes or expectations even then, as teenagers, about roles of men and women at home, in the workplace, in the world.

It was an amazing weekend that culminated when teens invited their parents to hear what they had learned. Students voted on and presented the information they were most afraid to talk about with their parents. Lastly, each student paired up with their parent(s) in a different corner of the room to talk about whatever topic they most wanted to address.

My Mama's Generation

My mother never took a sexuality course nor did she see any videos in high school about sex nor did she learn anything about sex from her mother. She had sex with one man: my father. I don't know if it first happened before or after she was married. She never told me. For the most part, mothers of the '50s and '60s were homemakers (see Did You Know for some Fun Facts). They were too busy pleasing their husbands and shushing their children to share stories with their teenage girls. I was trained to follow in my mother's footsteps. My home education included all of the skills taught to my mother by her mother and her home economics teacher such as cooking and sewing. My mother was competent and open for questions in these areas. She did not, however, encourage conversations about boys, kissing, sex, or a multitude of other uncomfortable topics.

In fact, my mother was taught *not* to communicate, and the skills of non-communication were passed on to me. Indirectly, I was taught to always *listen*, that my words were never as important as the other person's. I was taught not to complain or bother others with unimportant details about my day. If people took advantage of my time or were rude or unkind, it was understandable because of their circumstances or the stress in their lives. I was taught never to question the judgment of others or their integrity. Men and husbands, especially, should not be questioned about their actions since they would always be fair and truthful.

Did You Know / Fun Facts

About The 1950s

Roles of Women in the 1950s
(from a 1950s high school home economics textbook!)

- Have dinner ready. Plan ahead to have a delicious meal ready on time for your husband's return.

- Prepare yourself. Take 15 minutes to rest so you'll be refreshed when he arrives. Touch up your makeup, put a ribbon in your hair and be fresh-looking.

- Prepare the children. Take a few minutes to wash the children's hands and faces (if they are small), comb their hair and if necessary, change their clothes. They are little treasures and he would like to see them playing the part.

- Minimize all noise. At the time of his arrival, eliminate all noise of the washer, dryer, or vacuum. Try to encourage the children to be quiet.

- Greet him with a warm smile and show sincerity in your desire to please him.

- A good wife always knows her place.

Did You Know / Not-So-Fun Facts

About the 2000s

Roles/Stereotypes of the 2000s

- Only 10% of top management positions in S&P 500 companies are held by women.

- Only 4.8% of Fortune 500 companies are run by women.

- Women still get paid 70 cents on the dollar compared to men.

- 53% of 13-year-old girls and 78% of 17-year-olds are unhappy with their bodies.

- 65% of women have eating disorders and 17% of teens engage in cutting and other self-injury behaviors.

- Less than 50% of boys and men with mental challenges seek help because they feel shamed or humiliated for not being able to "man up."

- Teens receive stereotypical messages about roles of men and women every week because they spend 10 hours and 45 minutes a day consuming media:

  - 31 hours a week watching TV

  - 17 hours a week listening to music or watching music videos

  - 3 hours a week watching movies

  - 4 hours a week reading magazines

  - 10 hours a week online

Your Story

Even when teens are asked today—like my sons were in their sexuality course—to describe characteristics or sexuality of a man and woman, here were some of the gut reactions:

"Men are strong, tall, aggressive, masculine, tough, athletic, confident, optimistic, watch sports, play rough, don't cry and are the main financial providers."

"Women are beautiful and feminine, have long hair, wear makeup, wear dresses, are housewives, are sensitive, cry often, are not athletic, love cooking and decorating, are creative, have babies and are the main caretakers."

Teens weren't oblivious to the fact that many of the adjectives that first came to mind when describing roles of men and women were stereotypes, and not necessarily true for many people today. They realized the importance of breaking the stereotypes. When asked to give a more realistic description of guys and girls, I heard:

"Guys have different body parts, physical attributes, hormones. They all have different personalities, likes, and dislikes. They may be athletic, but they may be more creative and artistic. They may have a guy's body, but end up having a sex change later, so their body doesn't really end up meaning that much."

"Girls have different body parts. Many don't like dolls and would prefer to play in the dirt. Society planted the images of how they should act and what they should be, but they can do their own thing. We're all human, so there's no point in gender roles."

Some of these reactions came from YouTube videos I watched or articles I read, and some came from teens who sat in front of me in my classrooms or interviews. Most acknowledged that gender roles have changed even in their lifetimes and, in general, people have become more accepting and more open to all kinds of gender roles. They say there is less pressure, more education, and more bully prevention. They talked about television shows like *This Is Us*, *Blackish*, *The Fosters*, and *Modern Family* that fight gender roles and stereotypes. These sitcoms show sensitive dads, female breadwinners, multi-ethnic families, lesbian or gay parents. They show individuals fighting their own stereotypes about what men and women should think, how they should act, and what kinds of jobs they should hold.

Teens are some of the smartest people I know. They are aware of how far we still have to go. There is a movement that has begun following Emma Watson's address to the United Nations on feminism and the "He for She" movement. The movement is based on a definition of feminism as equality in rights and freedom for all humans. Some of the lines from her speech have been repeated in videos and memes:

"I believe . . .

* that women should be paid the same as males.
* that I should be able to make decisions about my own body.
* there should be more women in politics to speak on my behalf.
* that socially women should have the same respect as men."

Students brought up videos that, as a result of that speech, have gone viral. Young girls are asked to "run like a girl." The girls run as fast as they can, pumping their arms with smiles on their faces. One girl says, "I run like a girl because I'm amazing and fast." One girl says, "Catch up, people!" One video features a boy sharing that he doesn't fit the stereotype of strong guys and masculinity. He says that guys often want closeness just like girls do, but don't know how to show it because of the messages they get from society. Guys wear masks and are taught not to value caring and empathy.

Teens from all of my sources talked about both negative and positive messages sent through commercials, advertising, music videos, and other media outlets.

Negative Messages:

* Beer commercials still show men as being macho and masculine, watching sports and being waited on by women. There may be a man who is not watching the game or is helping his wife, but he is ridiculed and shown as emasculated.
* Commercials about cleaning products often feature women happily cleaning toilets and floors in traditional female roles of "housekeeper."

* Commercials for television products and even pizza show men in dominant decision-making positions and women following their instructions.

* Women are shown in car and motorcycle commercials, sexily clad, hair blowing in the breeze, fully made-up. The ads target men, but objectify women as sex objects.

Positive Messages:

* Girls can now see themselves on television in powerful positions like news anchors, politicians, doctors, firefighters, engineers, lawyers, scientists, and police officers, to name a few. Media can create consciousness that new leaders will look like women of all cultures and colors.

* There are more commercials showing men cleaning their homes or dads being the at-home caretakers.

* More gender-neutral toys are being promoted, and toys and games previously targeting only boys or only girls have begun to gear products to the opposite sex. For example, Legos has a set targeting girls that include science figures and non-sexist colors. Boys are targeted more as chefs in cooking sets previously only targeted to girls.

I interviewed Natalia, a senior only five months away from graduation. I wanted to know if she agreed that teens today still fight stereotypes about sexual roles. Natalia talked about her Hispanic culture and the concept of *machismo*. "Males have all the power. All my cousins and family members believe that males are taken care of by females. My dad was abusive and had the mindset that women have their role."

Natalia gave me a little background on her dad.

"He left when I was five and my brother was in middle school. Dad was an illegal immigrant and had accumulated parking tickets, so he ended up in jail with a four- to five-year sentence. When he left, he said to my brother, 'You're the man of the house now.'"

Natalia told me what happened in her home after her dad left, and what her older sister did to change the sexual roles and stereotypes in their home.

"My brother was twelve years old and the only male in our household. We girls were expected to cook for him, clear the table after he ate, clean his room, and do his laundry. My father never returned to our home after his sentence. He cheated on my mother and created a new family."

Natalia sees her oldest sister, Alandra, as an activist. Alandra coached both Natalia and their mother, "Your role is not just cooking and cleaning. You are powerful women. You don't need a man to succeed." Natalia said, "She had a saying, '*Lo estas manteniendo*,' which means, 'He's leeching off you.'" Natalia shared that Alandra had the mindset of a straight-A student, but felt pressured by their circumstances. She had an emotional breakdown at one point and told her mom, "No disrespect, but you didn't finish middle school. The government supports us, and it's up to me to make different choices."

When Natalia's brother turned eighteen, her mother realized that she didn't like the way she had raised him. She told him, "I want to teach you so you can take care of yourself." Natalia explained, "My mom began to change the way she handled my brother. When he finished eating and left his dishes on the table, my mom would say, 'What are you doing?' He would answer, 'I'm going to watch TV.' My mom would say, 'No, clear your table.' He would say, 'No, my sisters will do it.' My mom would answer, 'No, your sisters will take care of themselves.'"

Natalia described a day in the laundromat when her mother had decided it was time for the man of the house to do his own laundry.

"My brother had never been in a laundromat. I had been in

laundromats since I was very young. I had to teach him everything. It was never his responsibility. At first, he was angry, but later he joined the military and he came home and told my mom, 'I'm glad you taught me how to take care of myself.' Now he has a girlfriend that holds him accountable too. My mother's culture had taught her that the man will always be the alpha, but she realized that her ideas would no longer work for the next generation."

As a result of these changes, Natalia is proud that her siblings have succeeded in setting goals and reaching them. Her brother joined the Marines. Her oldest sister graduated from Berkeley. Her next sister is attending the University of Hawaii, double majoring in political science and ethnic studies.

Natalia takes AP classes, has a 4.1 GPA, commits to multiple clubs, and is taking college classes. She says, "I want to accomplish these goals for my sisters." In the ninth grade, she went to UCSD for a three-week program where she lived in the dorms and took college classes. In tenth grade, she went to the University of Arizona for a hands-on experience in ecosystems and ocean biospheres.

All of Natalia's accomplishments, along with her mother's willingness to allow her to pursue dreams traditionally only filled by men, reflect positive changes in gender norms in her family. She knows that she will also have to fight her role in society as an immigrant woman who does not yet have legal status. "If the Dream Act ends, how will I go to college? I'm not ready for the reality. I cried when I turned seventeen because I know there is not much time left. I'm still a woman. I'm still this color."

What I Wish My Mama Would Have Told Me

I wish my mama would have told me that my gender doesn't only have to do with sex. It is also about my role as a woman in society. It's about my abilities, my passions, my dreams for the future. It's about realizing that I can choose a job that I am qualified for, that I have gone to school for, or that I have a natural tendency towards, whether or not that job has traditionally been held by men.

I wish my mama would have shared what the matriarchs of our families had to go through so I could have better understood my own femininity. This strong generation of women found ways to survive in the world without much information.

I wish my mama would have told me that information gives me choices, and I can choose not to be around (or certainly date or marry) a man who objectifies women.

Opportunities to Journal

* What are the messages you have received from family or society that you must act a certain way, pursue a certain career, or not pursue a certain career because you are a girl?
* List some negative and positive points about being a girl.
* How can you help change the stereotypes that exist about roles of women and men? What does society still need to do to change the stereotypes that exist about roles of women and men?

Take-Aways

* Our sex is generally defined by whether we were born male or female. Gender has to do with how we express traits that traditionally may have been seen as male or female. Gender roles change over time based on cultural norms.
* Our ideas about sex and gender roles come from magazines, TV, social media, parents, and society.
* Roles of men and women have changed over time. Women are called to take an active part in creating the change that is still needed when identifying the roles of men and women in society.
* Stereotypes exist about the roles of men and women. For example, men are strong, tall, aggressive, masculine, athletic, and

confident, while women are sensitive, feminine, emotional, and creative.

* In truth, guys and girls have different body parts, physical attributes, and hormones. They have different personalities, likes and dislikes. Both may be athletic, creative, or artistic. Girls may have a tendency to be strong and dominant, while guys may be more sensitive and be better caretakers.

* Gender roles and stereotypes are being challenged today in television programs, commercials, movies, and on social media. Campaigns like "Run-like-a-girl" and "He for she" are shared in videos and memes. Girls can now see themselves in powerful positions like those held by women like Oprah Winfrey and Kamala Harris. They can imagine themselves in jobs traditionally held by men.

* Teen girls challenge cultural stereotypes in their own families by teaching female siblings, "Your role is not just cooking and cleaning. You are powerful women. You don't need a man to succeed." Male siblings are taught, "You can take care of yourself."

Chapter 6

Stress: Bad Effects & Better Choices

Do you ever feel so stressed that you think your eyeballs are going to pop out of your head? Maybe you're worried about school or parents or friends or enemies or money or family problems... and sometimes it's just too much to bear. There is so much to consider every day. It's overwhelming.

Over the years, I must have blocked out the parts of high school that were stressful because at first when I tried to remember them, all I could think of were the "normal" stresses like homework and grades. Yet, the more I thought about it, the more I remembered: A friend who struggled with an eating disorder. A girl in the bathroom passed out on drugs. When my best friend tried to take her life. The constant fights and stresses with my boyfriend.

When I talked to current teens, I found that some of you also experience issues I knew nothing about in high school, like immigration, social media bullies or predators, and very real fears about safety, meals, and whether dreams can ever come true. Let's identify and talk about those stresses, then and now. We'll look at eating disorders, self-injury, and anxiety disorders. Afterwards, we'll talk about ways to combat them.

Did You Know / Not-So-Fun Facts

Dealing with Stress in Unhealthy Ways

Eating Disorders:

Abnormal or disturbed eating habits that stem from an obsession with food, body weight, or body shape and often result in serious health consequences, including death. We're going to focus on teen girls because they have double the stats of teen guys.

Anorexia Nervosa	Teens with anorexia view themselves as overweight even when they're not. They often monitor their weight, avoid eating certain types of foods and severely restrict their calories.
Bulimia Nervosa	Teens with bulimia frequently eat unusually large amounts of food in a short period of time. They then attempt to purge to compensate for the calories by forced vomiting, fasting, laxatives, diuretics, enemas, and/or excessive exercise.
Binge Eating Disorder	Binge eating disorder is similar to bulimia except the teen does not purge, restrict calories, or exercise. Teens with this disorder are often overweight or obese. This may increase their risk of heart disease, stroke and type 2 diabetes.

Self-Injury Disorders:

Nonsuicidal self-injury is the act of deliberately harming the surface of your own body. The disorder includes cutting, burning, scratching, carving words or symbols on the skin, hitting or punching, piercing the skin with sharp objects, pulling out hair, or persistently picking at or interfering with wound healing.

Suicide Risk:

Although people with self-injury disorders and eating disorders are not necessarily trying to end their lives, there is also a risk of suicide because of the emotional problems that trigger self-injury or abusing one's body through unhealthy eating patterns. Teens with any of the above disorders (and more that are not listed) find it difficult to cope with their psychological pain. They have a hard time expressing or understanding emotions. There may be feelings of worthlessness, loneliness, panic, anger, guilt, rejection, self-hatred, or confused sexuality.

Generalized Anxiety (Stress) Disorder (GAD):

People with GAD experience intense worry and fear that may be greater than the situation calls for. Teens may worry about future events, past behaviors, social acceptance, family matters, personal abilities, school performance. All teens have some anxiety. It is a normal part of growing up. But sometimes worries and fears don't go away. They may interfere with normal daily life. In these cases, an anxiety disorder may be present.

Seeking Help:

If you recognize any of these emotions or disorders in yourself or a friend, please check the **Resources** section at the end of the book to find comfort and community. You can also try:

- Talking to a school counselor or calling a mental health specialist.

- Calling a suicide hotline number. In the U.S., call the National Suicide Prevention Lifeline at 1-800-273-TALK (1-800-273-8255).

- Calling a warm line in your area (https://warmline.org). A warm line is an alternative to a crisis line (hotline) that is run by "peers," generally those who have had their own experiences of trauma and are willing to share them (see **Resources**).

- Talking to your primary doctor or other health care provider.

- Reaching out to a close friend or loved one.

- Contacting a spiritual leader or someone else in your faith community.

My Story

Like conversations about sex and sexuality, conversations about stress were pretty nonexistent for my generation. It was understood that whenever bad stuff happened, we could and would "handle it." It's not that there wasn't stress; it just wasn't really acknowledged. Some of the unhealthy ways of dealing with stress weren't even named for teens yet. The "Did You Know" chart names many unhealthy ways to deal with stress. Naming is power. Without knowing what we're talking about, there are only secrets... and secrets are stressful.

My friend Gail went to high school during the '70s, like me. Beginning in high school, continuing through college, and for a good part of her life, Gail experienced anorexia nervosa, bulimia nervosa, binge eating, panic disorders, and suicidal ideations.

Gail's father worked countless hours as a college professor. Her mom graduated from college, but experienced mental health issues and insecurities. Gail was the firstborn and remembers feeling responsible for her mother's happiness, well-being, and emotional support from a very young age.

Gail said, "I learned years later in therapy, alone and with my mother, that her main goal as a parent was that I like her. Even as a toddler, my mom would take me to the park in hopes that I would make friends for *her*. She wanted me for herself, as her best friend.

"Girls constantly bullied me, beginning when I was in the third grade, probably because of my extreme shyness. I had no strategies to cope, and no friend except my mom. Sometimes she would let me stay home from school so that I didn't have to face my problems. We lived across the street from the school, and at recess, I would go to the fence nearest my house and yell, 'Mama!' She would come out of the house, cross the street, and be my friend during recess instead of teaching me skills to make friends and be on my own."

All of these early scenes were the underpinnings of Gail's eating disorders for the next thirty years. In high school, she gained weight. Her father noticed and made derogatory comments. She was still shy and a loner. At about fifteen years old, she went to a health food store and bought protein shakes. For breakfast and lunch, she drank a protein shake, and only ate a regular meal at dinnertime. She lost thirty pounds and grew several inches during the same short period of time.

"I received lots of compliments. It was intoxicating. The more compliments I received, the less I ate. I still went to school with the same girls that had bullied me. They grew out of teasing me, but I held a grudge and never forgave them. I continued to isolate. I completed 500 sit-ups every night before bed, and continued to lose weight."

When Gail's parents saw that she was losing significant weight, they told her that it was time to stabilize. She was not to lose any more weight. They made her step on the scale once a week in front of them. The night before she was to be weighed, she would eat more than usual. The rest of the week she hardly ate. Her aunt held a Ph.D. in child psychology; she told Gail's mom that Gail had a condition called anorexia nervosa. Gail remembers being proud to hold the title.

At 5' 8", Gail's weight was 135, which her parents said was the lowest "reasonable" weight they would allow. She lost her periods for a year, and her hair began to fall out. The summer between her junior and senior year of high school, Gail spent abroad in Europe. She wasn't being watched, and she didn't have a scale. Her lanky, thin body and long blonde hair gained her positive attention in Europe. By the time she stepped off the plane in the United States three months later, she weighed 109 pounds. Her mother burst into tears... not because she missed her. Girls with anorexia nervosa often view themselves as "fat" no matter how thin they are; Gail only saw weight gain when she looked in the mirror.

Gail gained ten pounds for her senior photo, weighing in at 118 pounds. She had never gone to a party or been on a date. She didn't go to her senior prom or her grad night. She continued to be painfully shy and unforgiving of any potential friends because of how they had treated her in the third grade. She looked forward to college as an opportunity to meet a new set of friends. She set off for Cal Poly, San Luis Obispo.

During her first semester, Gail gained forty pounds. She came home for winter break and her dad said, "You know, you don't have to eat everything on the plate." When she returned to school, she became eating partners with a girl who taught her how to eat and purge (see Bulimia Nervosa). They planned their meals together, and then ate and threw up four times a day. After meeting a boy and leaving her friend behind in the middle of her sophomore year, she was able to get her eating disorders under control for the next fifteen years.

Gail returned to eating disorders to handle her stress when she was in her late thirties, binge eating and contemplating suicide. She found a therapist who specialized in eating disorders. Her therapist told her, "When you were anorexic and bulimic, you were trying to draw people in and create a personal world. When you were binge eating, you were creating armor to protect yourself." Gail describes the process her therapist used as walking Gail backward through her childhood. She told Gail that the force behind her eating disorders was the stressful relationship with her mom. Gail answered, "What do you mean? She's my best friend."

The stress related to eating disorders can come both before and after the disorder. A girl can have a stressful relationship with her mother or another family member and/or experience general stress at home, school, or work. Those stresses can influence or lead to an eating disorder. On the other hand, once a girl has an eating disorder, there can be severe physical stresses on the body, which can cause more mental stress. A girl might constantly be worried about her food habits and weight, and at the same time battle emotions of guilt, anxiety, low self-esteem, and depression.

It took Gail many years after high school to face her eating disorders and to get healthy. Today she looks forward to driving trips she takes alone. She says, "I drive instead of fly because I want to face my fears. I drive through the areas that caused me the most grief to show myself that I survived."

Your Story

Some problems have not changed for teens over the years like stresses from parents and teachers. Teens still fight and will always fight stressors like weight loss or gain, hormone changes, rapid growth spurts, menstrual periods, and acne to name a few. They will always need at least nine hours of sleep and get only six or seven, depending on their homework and extracurricular activities. They will always have emotions that may overwhelm them and make them feel sad, angry, frustrated, or tired. They will sometimes skip meals or eat less than healthy food when they are rushing from school to practice to home, and then back to school for an evening sport or activity.

But there are stressors that teens have today that Gail and I didn't have. Technology has changed everything. Sometimes it makes life easier and sometimes it creates more stress. We've already talked about some of these issues in **Chapter 4**. There are stresses that are hard to see or control when teens are on sites like Facebook, Instagram, or Twitter, internet searches gone wrong, and cell phone texts. People are more likely to make comments on the computer or phone that they would never say in person. Even bullying is no longer necessarily done face to face, and students sometimes cannot find solace in their own home or bedroom.

There is a spectrum of teen responsibility and stress. Some teens, especially those who may have parents working late nights or early mornings, may have the responsibility to cook and care for younger siblings in addition to the responsibilities of their homework and extracurricular activities.

I interviewed just such a teenager. Her name is Jessica. We met in the library of her high school over two afternoons. At the first meeting, when we talked about the subject of stress, she told me about the pressure she feels as the oldest of three children in her family. She maintains a high GPA and takes AP courses. She said, "I am always trying to manage my time, and I do think that stress has affected my mental health." She shared that at high times of stress, she isolates by staying in her room and not hanging out with friends and family. She sleeps less and continuously makes lists in her head. At the same time, she can't understand why her friends complain about family responsibilities. She said, "My friends get to go out, but I have to watch my siblings. I might think to myself, *Why is this my responsibility? They're my parents. They should be watching my young siblings.* But I would never let my parents know I feel that way because I don't want them to think I'm ungrateful. It's what I can give back to my family."

In our second interview, we discussed stress again. I wanted to know if she thought that any of the expectations from her family were cultural. At first, she didn't answer. Instead she said, "At a very young age, I knew what would upset my parents. I wanted to keep my parents content. I didn't want to add to their problems. I also didn't have any issues with hanging out with my sisters." When I continued to ask whether these extra responsibilities at home might add to the stress she felt to accomplish all of her scholastic goals, she began to tell me her family story.

Her mother and father emigrated from Mexico when she was just a baby, and are undocumented. That makes her a DACA (Deferred Action for Childhood Arrivals) student. Her two younger siblings were born in the United States, so they are legal citizens. Though she said, "I know I can make it," she also acknowledged that her parents' legal status gives her doubts about whether she can attain her education goals. And then she shared with me the worry list she had referred to in our first meeting:

* *Some colleges or potential jobs won't accept me without a social security number. After I go to college, my status may also affect what kind of job I can get.*
* *I have to focus on getting there. I have to wait it out, and see what happens with the Dream Act.* (Note: The Dream Act allows young

undocumented immigrants permanent resident status for up to eight years and protects them from deportation.)

* *I may be able to go to school and work, but on the other hand, the programs may be eliminated. My resources may disappear depending on the laws.*

She paused in her list at this point and told me about a day eight months before when ICE (Immigration and Customs Enforcement) detained her father:

My dad left our apartment to go to work early one morning. We were all getting ready to go to school. He called my mom a few minutes later. I overheard the one-sided conversation.

"Where are you? All right. I'm coming."

I could tell something was wrong by the tone of my mom's voice.

I asked her, "Where are you going?"

"They have your dad. I'm going to go see what's going on. Call your grandma."

I found out later that ICE officers were in a car outside waiting for him. I texted my aunts because I didn't have a number for my grandma. I was in shock. I broke down crying. My thoughts were all over the place. I thought to myself, Is this going to be the moment where everything is going to change?

My mom wasn't answering texts. I found out later she was on the phone, maybe with a lawyer. Dad was already taken away. He had unlocked his phone for the ICE officers, and they had called my mom. They gave her two options: 1) We can come and get you too, or 2) You can turn yourself in. They told her that either way, they both would be back home the same day. My grandma came and took us to school. All day, I was thinking about what might happen to our family. I couldn't concentrate. I didn't think anyone would know details, so I didn't text family members.

My head was full: Who is going to look after my sisters? Will I have to stop going to school? My life will be completely different. I'll have to go back to Mexico. I won't be able to accomplish everything I planned for my future. My sisters are only ten and six, but they are citizens so they should stay in the U.S. Moving to Mexico would not give them as much opportunity. They will grow up unhappy. They'll have to stay with foster parents or extended family.

My mom texted me in the afternoon. She said, "I'm going to turn myself in. I promise I will be out by the end of the night." I felt calmer, but I was still worried. After school, my grandma picked me up and we picked up my sisters and went home. We gave them a simple explanation, "Mom and Dad will be home later." I think they would have had more questions if I hadn't been there. My presence kept them calm. This time we were fortunate that both parents were home by the end of the day.

The first few months after the incident, I couldn't think or talk about it without crying.

At this point in the interview, I struggled to see Jessica clearly through my own tears. I asked her, "How are you not crying right *now?*" She said, "I can't stay in that place of fear, or I would not be able to go to school, maintain my grades, take care of my siblings, and reach my dreams."

I am awed by this young woman and many like her right now in schools all over our country. I don't know the solutions to the immigration questions facing our country today, but I do know that young women are facing huge challenges and stresses every day. These stressors aren't going away, so let's see what we can do to make your lives a little more manageable.

Sometimes the stresses become more than we can bear. I interviewed a girl named Lexi whose friend, Jeanne, was cyberbullied and physically bullied. They were desk partners in their Human Body Systems class.

One day in class Jeanne said, "Lexi, can I tell you something?"

"Yeah, of course."

"I've been cutting myself. I'm scared."

She showed me new, barely healed scars.

She whispered, "I don't know how I can live life anymore. My boyfriend is telling me I'm useless, hopeless, ugly, not worth anything."

I thought to myself, Why is she telling me this? Why me?

As if she heard my thoughts, she said, "You're the only person who has not gone behind my back. You don't see color. You bring positivity. You bring people up."

We worked for a while on our project and then Jeanne said, "I want to kill myself. I don't want to live another day."

Inside I said, She's telling me this for a reason; otherwise she wouldn't be telling me.

Out loud I said, "Are you planning to do this today?"

"Today when I get home from school."

I stayed cool-headed. I was imagining scenarios.

I asked her, "What are you doing during lunch?"

"I'll be alone."

I wanted to get her to my favorite teacher's room so I could get some help.

"Come with me to Ms. Woodfill's room. Lots of us eat lunch there. It's really cool. We share our food and have a picnic. We're going to talk about TV shows. It's a safe environment with safe friends. There are no abusive friends."

She agreed to come. We loaded up our backpacks, and I had a second to say to a mutual friend, "Help me take her to Ms. Woodfill's room."

I thought, Breathe. Act normal. Make her feel comfortable.

We ate, and lunch was about over. I said, "I'm going to the bathroom," and went outside the classroom, motioning Ms. Woodfill to come with me. I told her what was going on and that my friend wanted to take her life.

When lunch was over, Ms. Woodfill casually said to her, "How are you doing? You seem kind of down." They talked, and Ms. Woodfill took her to the nurse. I found out later that her mom picked her up and took her to the hospital.

After it was all over and she was feeling well again, my friend said to me, "You are the person who saved my life. I told you for a reason." She is in college now and doing well.

Lexi did everything right that day to protect her friend. She stayed calm, didn't leave her friend alone, went to a safe place, and found a trusted adult to get more help than she could provide. We all have the ability to be there for someone else in need, because we know how it feels to be exhausted, overwhelmed, and abandoned. I know I would want a friend like Lexi if I was at my lowest moment, and I know I would want to be a friend to someone who couldn't see any options or hope. We can be each other's strength when times are tough.

How Teens Relieve Stress

I asked every teen I interviewed how he or she relieved stress. Jessica, from the first story, said, "One of my teachers has taught us to do meditation circles and something called *The 60 Seconds Fix.* She allows us to take a minute or two as needed to literally take a deep breath. I also walk my dogs and play with my two-year-old brother. I try to approach stress differently by writing it down, getting it out of my head." Lexi, from the second story, said, "I talk to my teacher, Ms. Woodfill, and academy director, Ms. Hohenstein."

> The 60 Seconds Fix *gives students an opportunity to stop for 60 seconds when feeling stressed, take a deep breath to "ground" themselves, and become aware of their body and mind so they can be fully present (see **Resources**).*

I found that teens who had learned ways of coping with stress often had adult role models they could turn to.

Here's a list of "fixes" I heard about from other interviewees:

* ❉ I surround myself with people who love me and understand me.
* ❉ I try to remember that stress is temporary, but the results of my hard work and reaching my goals will bring me serenity and happiness.
* ❉ Cleaning and organizing calms me.
* ❉ I hug my dog and listen to music.
* ❉ I play the flute, piccolo, cello, clarinet; these instruments are my main coping mechanism.
* ❉ I say the affirmation, "I can do it." Then I can manage all the feelings I am experiencing.
* ❉ I look for positive people, and radiate positivity and strength.

Here are a few of my own:

* ❉ Eat a little. Some protein in the morning before you go to school: an egg, some nuts, some dark green veggies, some dark red or purple fruits.
* ❉ Move a little. If you aren't already an athlete, try to string together a few weeks of a little more movement. You may find that you start to feel a little more energetic, a little more satisfied with who you see in the mirror.
* ❉ Sleep a lot. Snuggle in your favorite blanket and get just a little more sleep.
* ❉ Take care of yourself. You are a miraculous creature. You deserve it.

What I Wish My Mama Would Have Told Me

My mother didn't know about all of the negative ways teens were beginning to handle ever-increasing stress, but I wish she would have told me that my feelings and my fears and my insecurities were real. I wish she would have told me that if I ever felt like my life was spinning out of control, I could come to her.

I wish we would have had conversations about all of the stressors of my teenage life. I wish I would have known that I was the most important person in my life. My eating, sleeping, and moving habits were important to keep me safe and healthy. And that no activity, no grade, no friend, no insecurity, no stress was worth jeopardizing my beautiful self.

Opportunities to Journal

* What aspects of your life cause you stress?
* What are some ways you could take care of yourself, starting today, that would help relieve your stress?
* What are adjustments you may need to make in your daily schedule to make you healthier and happier?
* In what ways do you relate to girls who have issues with their weight, eating habits, or other emotional problems?

Take-Aways

* Stress can cause you to deal with your problems in unhealthy ways, like eating disorders, self-injury disorders, and worse.
* Stress can look like being bullied, shamed, humiliated, or over-protected by a parent or family member. Stress can look like never being satisfied with who/what you see when you look in the mirror.
* The stress related to eating, self-injury, or general stress disorders can come before and after the disorder. A girl can engage in a risky disorder because she is stressed, and once she is engaged in the disorder, she can experience severe physical stresses on the body. In addition, she will likely battle emotions of guilt, anxiety, low self-esteem, and depression.
* There is help for you in friends, teachers, counselors, doctors, spiritual leaders, and help lines. As a result of stress, you may even consider taking your own life. There are many people who care. Reach out. Call a friend. Tell an adult. Get help. You are worth it (see **Resources**).

* Learn to relieve your stress in small ways like playing with an animal, listening to music, taking a walk, calling a friend. Surround yourself with positive friends, family, and role models. Try to eat a little healthier, exercise a little more, and sleep a lot more.

Chapter 7

Creativity Matters

Have you ever been stuck on what to write for a paper due in English class? You stared at the paper or the computer screen and your mind wandered off to your boyfriend, what you'll wear tomorrow, or the awkward moment with your best friend during lunch? Maybe you took a break to finish the amazing book you were reading, or to listen to an album by a new artist you love or an inspirational TED Talk, or to complete a difficult equation for math class. Maybe you went back to the English paper and something had shifted in your creative brain. An idea came to you, and you ran with it.

It's understood now—backed by research—that doing something creative can open up paths in your brain that lead you to new answers and possibilities in every subject. Creativity isn't just about having talents like singing or dancing or athletic ability. It's about accessing the knowledge within each of us to create (like a poem or a musical piece) or to solve problems (like global warming, recycling, overpopulation, or saving the earth's resources). In fact, our creativity can be most engaged when solving complex problems that have no easy solution, and typical ways of dealing with them may not work.

Creativity matters because it reduces stress and develops confidence and emotional health. It helps provide focus for problem-solving, often in unconventional ways. And at the end of the day, no matter what direction you decide to go in your life, you can take your creativity with you to help you cope with and express feelings. Creativity can open your heart to new ways of seeing and thinking. Ultimately, creativity can increase feelings of accomplishment and satisfaction in whatever path you choose.

My Story

When I was a teen, I thought of creativity as visual arts like painting or sculpting, musical arts like singing or playing instruments, written arts like poetry, short stories, and journalism, and physical arts like dancing or drama. These kinds of creative endeavors brought me joy and helped relieve my teen stress, for sure.

But I did not think creativity was part of math or science or physics. In my personal experience, core subjects were boring and difficult, and I didn't understand or like all the rules and laws I had to obey. Scientists and visionaries from the past like Albert Einstein, Thomas Edison, and the Wright brothers dropped out of high school, partly because they chose not to be confined. Women scientists from the same time period like Marie Curie—two-time winner of the Nobel Prize in both Physics and Chemistry—had to work even harder just to be noticed. More recent visionaries like Bill Gates, Steve Jobs, and Walt Disney did not do well in a structured environment either. Oprah Winfrey did well in school, but had to overcome difficult living situations, running away from home, and attending several different high schools. She excelled at public speaking and got her first job as a broadcaster at seventeen years old. We wouldn't know many of the facts we know today or have access to many of the inventions that have made our life more exciting, comfortable, and enjoyable if not for all of the creative people who have gone before us.

Before my own teenage stress began, I grew up when children could still ride their bikes across town and safely stay out past dark in the neighborhood streets playing Hide and Seek, Hopscotch, and Flag Football. But beyond our own creative play, my mother gave my sisters and me multiple opportunities to try organized creative endeavors. First, we took ballet and tap. I stuck with tap for seven years. Then we took piano lessons. I stuck with that for four or five years. In sixth grade, I started playing my late grandfather's violin. I stuck with that for six years. I am grateful to my parents for giving me all those opportunities to try on different creative endeavors.

One more activity I enjoyed was writing. My father helped me write an epic poem one day while he was painting and antiquing some cabinets. It took us hours, and I felt like a creative genius. My father made sure I performed it for my mother and sisters at the end of our grand accomplishment. One day, Dad brought home a used typewriter for me from a shop next door to his shoe store. I felt ecstatic. I cut paper the size of most books I had read, and I began to write a book. I would insert piece after piece of the five-by-seven paper into the typewriter, putting together the chapters of each book. My girlfriend from down the street would work with me to come up with ideas. When each book was finished, we would put a cover on it and staple along the sides to create the binding. My ten-year-old self was passionate about being a writer.

Even with these opportunities, I had to fight against those gender roles we've already talked about. My mother thought it was important that I be prepared to be a mother, so I took home economics classes. She also thought it important that I be prepared to help support my family financially, so I took secretarial and typing classes. My creative passions were not as important to my family as the practicality of having a job that took care of my family. Today, creativity is becoming the very essence of what it will take to figure out solutions to every kind of problem in every kind of career.

Did You Know

How to Become More CREATIVE

C — **Communicate** ideas confidently using different technology. Collaborate with others. Challenge yourself with different problems to solve.

R — **Record** new ideas, concepts, attempts and failures without judgment. Reflect in solitude to recognize new connections and possibilities.

E — **Engage** with interesting and diverse people.

A — **Appreciate** traditional modes of creating such as visual and performing arts, but extend your appreciation to nontraditional creativity in every field.

T — **Think** critically and ethically from many different perspectives. Try new activities and skills in a variety of ways. Transform your understanding of the world and your response to it.

I — **Imagine** without limits. Include many disciplines together in the same project or solution (music, science, math, technology, language arts).

V — **View** problems with flexibility and adaptability to go beyond predictable answers.

E — **Envision** innovative solutions with curiosity, ingenuity and focus.

Why CREATIVITY Matters

R — **Reduces** stress and anxiety.

E — **Emotional** maturity and confidence is developed.

N — **Nontraditional** problem-solving skills are critical today.

E — **Expands** appreciation for beauty and discovery in every field.

W — **Work** in jobs of the future will rely on your ability to think unconventionally, question ideas and imagine new alternatives.

Your Story

The good news is that the kind of creativity we're talking about in this chapter isn't necessarily something we're born with. We often think that we either have a particular artistic ability or we don't. The kind of creativity we're talking about can be developed. We can learn to focus, and imagine and dream solutions to complex problems. We can combine subjects we love with subjects we don't love, and work with others who have different talents than we do until we create an entire new way of thinking. We can try on different ways of experiencing the world and its creativity and discard those that don't work for us.

The hard part about being a teen is that we often don't know where we want our creativity to take us yet, and we allow the unknowns to cause us stress. What if, instead, we used creativity to relieve some of the stress in our lives? Let's see how one student used the arts as an outlet to find some serenity and relief in the midst of her teen challenges.

I interviewed a senior named Roxanne who had a lot to say about how creativity in music saved her from an emotionally abusive stepfather and allowed her to concentrate in her academic classes so she could focus on her goal to be a doctor.

Her father left her mother when Roxanne was young, leaving her mother depressed and alone with four children. She shared:

In the fifth grade, my mother remarried. I got along with my stepdad for about a year before his toxic personality created constant conflict. I told myself, I'll be the bigger person. I'll be happy and positive. He won't stop me from being successful.

My stepdad drank on the weekends and cussed at me. He said, "I'll send you to an orphanage." I never wanted to go home. He would take my siblings to school and make me walk. He would pass me in the car and flip me off.

I would talk to myself and say, Roxanne, don't be like him. You see him? He's a good example of what not to be. Get your education. He didn't. He's a dishwasher, a nobody. Nobody to make you feel this way. *I protected my siblings. I helped them with their homework and took them to the park.*

My mom would not stand up for me. She said, "You're just a kid; you can't do anything about it." There was a gap between my family and me. No one could see how fake my stepdad was. I was the dramatic one, taking everything the wrong way. I stopped trusting my mom because she supported him. When I was at home, I refused to speak.

When I asked Roxanne how she survived these conditions in her own home, she said:

I learned how to be two people: one at home and one at school. I knew I had to find an outlet for my anger and frustration. One day I passed the band room and heard a student playing the flute. I thought it was the most beautiful sound I had ever heard. I asked the band director if I could learn to play. I connected with the flute and learned how to play it in two days. On the third day, my teacher moved me up to advanced. I learned to play the flute, piccolo, cello, and the clarinet.

Instruments are my main coping mechanism. Playing saved me. Playing instruments is my superpower. When I play, I turn everything else off, close my eyes, breathe, and play. The song flows through me. My superpower only works when I'm at my lowest. I can hear the emotion in the song. The instruments have personalities, and their sound talks to me. I close my eyes and pour it all out. I can forget about everything. When I'm at the bottom of the ocean, fighting for air, I can fight to the top.

As Roxanne developed her skill in playing instruments, she was able to block out the negatives in her life and develop skills in her academic subjects as well. Her creative outlet led to her decision to enter her school's Health and Science Academy as a step in becoming a doctor. She was able to maintain a rigorous study schedule and participate in internships that gave her experience for her chosen field.

It benefits us when we think of creativity in terms of its many 21st century components: Using imagination, focus, curiosity, ingenuity, innovation, communication, flexibility, failure, and collaboration to solve complex problems. If we are constantly using all of these creative parts of ourselves to decide who we are and who we want to be, we cannot help but be successful in our own definition of the word "success."

What I Wish My Mama Would Have Told Me

I wish my mama would have told me to keep creating. I wish she would have told me to focus on the practices that brought me joy, even while deciding my career path. I wish she would have told me that in order to stick with a passion of any kind, I might have to give up something else I loved that took away my focus. Maybe I'd have to give up a favorite TV show, an afternoon with a friend, long conversations on the phone, or another Nancy Drew novel. Sometimes, like in a garden, many healthy seedlings come up, but we have to pull some so that the remaining plants thrive.

I wish we would have had conversations about what I was good at and what my skills looked like. I wish I would have known that once I knew my strengths, I would need to grow my creativity and continually renew myself so that I could be of the most use to myself and my planet—not because my parents told me to—but because I couldn't really be who I was without doing that thing.

Opportunities to Journal

* What are your hobbies? How do your hobbies make you feel? How do they renew you and focus you?

* In what ways do you see creativity helping you in your future career?

* Do you sometimes feel like giving up on a certain activity or subject area? If so, how can you decide which activities and

subjects are really your passions and which ones you can give up?

* What form of creativity opens you up and makes you feel like you can do anything or survive anything? Explain.

Take-Aways

* Creativity opens up paths in your brain that lead you to new ways of seeing and thinking so that you can help solve complex global problems in every discipline/subject/field in unconventional ways.

* Creativity is about accessing the knowledge within you to create (like a poem or a musical piece) or to solve problems (like global warming, recycling, overpopulation, or saving the earth's resources).

* Creativity matters because it reduces stress and develops confidence and emotional health. Creative outlets give you ways to cope with daily life.

* Some creative skills can be developed by working with someone who loves a different subject than you, and then combining your skills to create a new way of thinking.

* Creativity can improve academic performance, motor skills, confidence, visual learning, decision-making, and general satisfaction for living.

Chapter 8

When Creativity & Passion Meet Career

Are you a person who has always known what you want to be when you grow up? Do you feel the most alive when running or playing soccer or singing or dancing or practicing your instrument? Are you the happiest when solving an equation or a puzzle? Do you love to draw or design structures? Maybe you are a person who likes to do a lot of things, but nothing has piqued your interest yet. Maybe you are at a point in your life where you just don't think you're good at anything right now. That's okay too.

Some teens, like Roxanne, who we met in the last chapter, know exactly what they want to do and have been working towards their goals since they were young . . . against all odds. Some teens (like me) get sidetracked many times, and have to keep listening to their hearts over and over again. Some will have to wait years to truly find where they fit in the scary, exciting, overwhelming, awesome landscape of today's job markets. Wherever you fit in these scenarios, you are a unique individual who will find your way.

My Story

I chose to marry my high school sweetheart when I was eighteen. I took legal secretary courses at a community college until, with the help of an instructor, I landed a job downtown in a legal office. Even though my passions were English literature and writing, I dropped out of community college to help my young husband pay the bills. (You'll hear more about my high school husband in future chapters.)

I finally returned to the same community college many years later, finished my general education requirements, and enrolled at San Diego State University. I was thirty-seven years old. I was going to be an English teacher. I felt as if a college education had been waiting for me my entire life.

San Diego State is a beautiful campus, fifteen miles from the beach and thirty miles from the mountains. It has its own rolling hills, tree-lined park, and gurgling waterfall. Just taking the first stroll across campus opened my mind to new possibilities. I encountered every color of skin, heard an abundance of languages, considered numerous new hairstyles, overheard genres of music and lyrics to which I'd never before been exposed. I was blinded by the "bling-bling" of piercings, nose rings, and diamond studs. I passed just as many students who were more subdued in jeans, flip-flops, tie-dyed shirts, and retro pea coats. I witnessed student protestors, political activists, studying intellectuals, and performing dramatists. Before I ever entered the classroom, I knew I would never be the same.

It took many years for me to find the excitement and passion I had left behind in high school. When I finally decided what I wanted to be when I grew up—and had the courage to pursue it—my life became more fulfilling. I am telling you this story because I want you to know that it's never too late to begin the rest of your life. We get do-overs as many times as we need!

My first teaching job after graduating from SDSU was in an inner-city high school that enrolled students from over thirty cultures speaking twice as many dialects. I continued to learn from my students over the next twenty years. Even though I had to wait many years to pursue my creativity and the career that went with it, I had more choices than the women who came before me. My grandmother went to college and earned a teaching credential in the early 1900s when most women did not have the opportunity. But instead of teaching, she married, stayed at home, and raised six children while her husband worked. I had more choices than my aunt, who stayed home with her four children while her husband worked and wished her mama (my grandmother) had told her she could be anything she wanted to be. After my grandfather died in his mid forties, my grandmother moved her six children to a different town and got a job at the county courthouse. Years later, my grandmother became the first woman County Recorder in South Dakota, and even then her daughters didn't get the message that they could be anything they wanted to be.

Your Story

Teens today have more choices than I did. In the classes I taught, we often talked about how career choices can be overwhelming, but I'm excited that young women can now choose occupations traditionally held only by men. They can join the military, be firefighters or police officers. They can be engineers or politicians, artisans or mechanics.

When working with senior students one of the final years of my teaching career, we completed a video/journal series called *Roadtrip Nation*. Students were given journals where they explored their talents and hobbies. They thought about what they were good at and what they loved to do. Then they made Venn diagrams to consider where those interests and passions might overlap. We had crazy brainstorming sessions where students created jobs using two or three of their passions at the same time. Students had to research folks in their own community doing something similar to the job they had created from their Venn diagram. Next, they interviewed those businesses, and prepared a presentation to fulfill their senior project.

Here is the blank slate where they each began:

How to Choose a Passion Career

Some things to consider when choosing a career:

- The three things you are **most passionate about** in life (like science, green industries and biology OR music, teaching and disabilities).

- Your own **personal qualities** such as dedication, perseverance and desire to learn, which are more important than any other aspect of choosing a career.

- The **values** around work that are most important to you (like high income, emotional engagement, prestige, belonging to a group, independence).

Tips/Options:

- Make a list of what you see as your natural gifts or strengths.

- Take a career interest quiz (The MAPP™, StrengthsQuest, Career Strengths Test).

- Take a personality test (Myers-Briggs or Strong Interest Inventory).

- Research careers (Use resources such as Occupational Outlook Handbook, CareersBox, Bright Knowledge, TotalProfessions).

- Talk to career advisors/counselors.

- Visit career fairs.

- Visit businesses that do what you want to do.

- Talk to people already doing what you want to do.

- Work for free at a location that houses your dream job!

- Ask for a paid internship that's somehow related to what you want to do.

- Whatever your passion is, keep practicing so you will be the best at it!

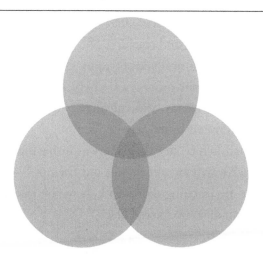

Choose three things you love to do. Put one in each circle of this Venn diagram. Now brainstorm how they overlap and fill in the center overlapping circles. What job did you create for yourself that includes all three of your passions?

One student—we'll call her Janet—had three bubbles: helping her community, dancing, and teaching. She knew that she wasn't the most consistent student academically, but she knew that she was a solid dancer, cared about others, was energetic and dedicated, and enjoyed teaching her friends difficult dance moves. She knew that she was more interested in helping her community and giving back to those who had helped her than she was in having a high-paying job in a city far away from her family and friends. She thought her ideal job would be teaching dance to kids in the inner city. Here's what Janet's Venn diagram looked like:

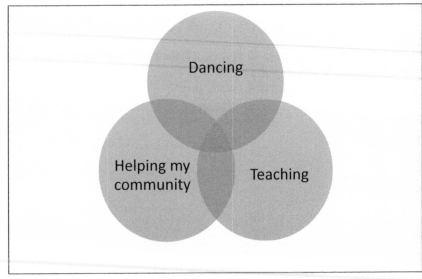

Janet researched dance facilities in the neighborhoods surrounding our high school and found a few. She made phone calls and set up interviews. Her favorite was a nonprofit organization where children and teens could go to express themselves through dance. Cost was based on family income, and no one was turned away. Dancers could also receive help with their homework and brainstorm their future education or job interests. She interviewed the director and delivered an awesome presentation to our class about her findings. Her personal qualities and values impressed the director, and she was offered a summer internship.

Another student—we'll call her Gina—had a difficult time getting through her four years of high school, wasn't planning to go to college, and just wanted this last project behind her so she could graduate. She liked to work alone, preferred to be inside rather than outside, and could get lost for hours in a good book or a video game. She didn't care if she ever made a huge amount of money, but her parents had made it clear that she had to find a way to support herself, especially if she wasn't going to college. Her Venn diagram bubbles looked like this:

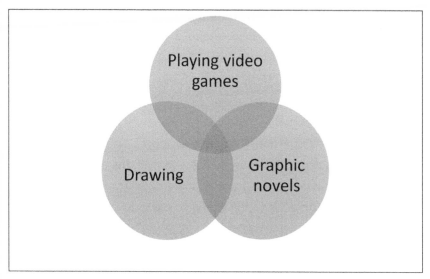

She thought her dream job could be to first draw characters, then create worlds for them to live in, and eventually design her own video games. Gina was overwhelmed with how she would find anyone to interview who would understand her unique situation. We brainstormed together, searched on the internet, and looked up local artists. She interviewed a graphic design nonprofit in San Diego, known for working with children and teens to create graphic novels and other artistic projects. Gina ended up being one of the students most excited about her project and felt like the future had opened a door to her.

What I Wish My Mama Would Have Told Me

I wish my mama would have had more conversations with me about my passions and what I wanted to be when I grew up. I wish she would have watched me more as I grew and observed what hobbies and subjects brought me joy. I wish she would have told me that money is not the only reason for choosing an occupation. When she saw me excelling in writing and reading, I wish she would have helped me realize that I was being drawn towards a calling, something I would love forever (not of the boyfriend type). I wish she would have said, "There is an occupation just for you, maybe one that has been calling you since the moment of your birth. Let me help you arrive there and thrive there." I wish that she would have told me that I could "do just fine" as a legal secretary, or I could spend my life smack dab in the middle of my greatest passion.

Opportunities to Journal

* What are your passions (art, music, sports, animals, computer games, socializing)? What makes you feel the most creative? What are you doing when you're in your bliss?

* What are your skills (science, math, computers, creative work, research)?

* What are your personal qualities (managing time, working with people, planning ahead, joining in discussions, caring for people, listening)?

* Brainstorm jobs that would fit into your skills and your passion. If you are having a difficult time with skills right now in your life, concentrate on what you are doing when you are happiest.

* What next steps do you want to take after high school? Education? Trade School? Military? Peace Corps or other community service?

Take-Aways

* Following your passion is not always easy and looks different for everyone.

* It's never too late to find a passion and pursue it. Do-overs are encouraged!

* You can now choose occupations traditionally held only by men. Join the military or be a first responder, an engineer, politician, artisan, or mechanic.

* There are many sources to help you choose what careers may fit with your skills and passions.

* Visiting different career sites, interviewing those who work there, volunteering, and interning can help you network and open up possibilities you could not imagine on your own.

* The three-circle Venn diagram is a great way to create your dream job so that you can live and thrive in a career that brings you joy!

Chapter 9

Follow Your Intuition; It's Never Too Late to Change Your Mind

Have you ever had a nagging sensation that someone was looking at you or following you? Has your heart ever raced because a stranger was approaching you, so you crossed the street or changed direction? Have you ever had a gut feeling that something wasn't safe, so you didn't ride in a certain friend's vehicle? Later you found out there was an assault on the street, or the friend you didn't ride with was in a car accident? When asked later how you knew to go/stop/turn/run, you said, "I don't know. I just knew." Or maybe you had the feeling and you didn't listen to it. Maybe something happened you regret, and later you said, "I knew I shouldn't have done that."

That "gut feeling experience" is called intuition. Intuition comes from everything we have learned and experienced from the time we were born. It comes from our family values and our memories. Our intuition comes from a deep sense of knowing, and is the wisest part of who we are. In times of stress or confusion, our intuition quickly knows the right thing to do based on the immediate circumstances. If we listen to this unexplainable feeling, this intuition that urges us to go this way or run that way, we can save ourselves from little aggravations and big mistakes.

My Story
My elementary school was smack dab in the middle between my house and my father's shoe store. Sometimes my big sister or one of

my parents would pick me up and walk me across the busy intersection to the shoe store. Sometimes I would walk to my house with other friends who lived in the same neighborhood. Either direction was about four blocks. On some days I came out of the school by myself and waited for friends, and other times I started walking and just met up with whomever was going my direction.

One day when I came out, a man was waiting in his car right in front of the school. He said, "Hi honey. I'm picking you up today." I kid you not, just like the stories of the boogeyman, he had a lollipop to entice me into his car. I got that itsy bitsy feeling in the pit of my stomach that something was unsafe. I did not second-guess that feeling or try to analyze it. I hadn't been scarred by peer pressure yet. I turned and ran like the wind back into the school, straight into the principal's office. An adult accompanied me outside to look for the car and the man with the lollipop; both had disappeared.

My parents made sure I was surrounded by friends or family for the next several days. But I do remember the first time I walked out of school alone again; that same man was parked in his car—across the street this time—and he did not have a lollipop. The lollipop was replaced by an evil scowl. He motioned me to get in his car. Maybe he thought if lollipops didn't work, anger would. I was not his daughter, and no amount of anger was going to get me to obey his command. I high-tailed it around, once again, and went for the principal's office. That was the last time I ever saw him. How ironic is it that I knew *exactly* how to take care of myself when I was a child, but lost that ability as a young woman.

Okay, here's another one. I was in middle school, walking home by myself. Usually my friend who lived on my street accompanied me, but she hadn't gone to school that day. I was walking along the main drag, two streets away from my street where I would turn right and head up the block to my house. I suddenly got a feeling that I was being followed. I squinted into my peripheral vision and saw a car slowly following behind me. My stomach churned and my heartbeat accelerated, yet I remember thinking about how embarrassing it would be to start running. After all, I didn't even know why the car was following me. Maybe the guy just needed directions. That gut feeling that tells us to protect ourselves at all costs—so pure when we are young—battled with my embarrassment. I was afraid to show my insecurities even to strangers.

The back door opened, and a man got out. I was even with the side street that came one street before my own, and there was no one in sight. I pretended there was someone there. I screamed, "Oh hey! I wondered where you were! Wait up!" and ran towards my ghost-friend. The screaming and the distraction were enough for the guy to jump back in the car and for the driver to race away. My instinct to save myself was alive and well, even though my desire to look cool had nearly changed my outcome.

We'll jump way into the future for stories when I *didn't* listen to my intuition at all. I didn't listen when I was sixteen and began to make relationship mistakes. I didn't listen when I was seventeen and my boyfriend asked me to marry him. I didn't listen when I broke out in hives the night before I married this man who would become an abusive cheater. Big, red blotches covered my neck, arms, and face. I screamed for my mother from my bedroom mirror where my splotchy face stared back at me, already contorted with tears. She came running down the hall. "Mom, I can't go to the rehearsal dinner! Look at me! I look like a strawberry and I'm getting puffier by the second! I can't get married tomorrow!" She, of course, comforted me and told me it was nerves. "Every bride gets nervous the day before her wedding. You look beautiful. Come sit in the kitchen with me. I'll get you a drink of water, and we'll just be calm and quiet until it's time to go." Before I left for the dinner, I changed into a sweater with a high neck. Thank God it was December.

The next day, my father made me stay home and relax all day

instead of helping to prepare the church and the reception hall for the evening wedding. He didn't want any more puffiness and tears. It was long before brides spent all day getting their hair and nails done, then riding around town in a limousine with their wedding party. I had hot curlers in my hair, and I painted my own nails. It was a cold day. My father kept a fire going in the fireplace, and I stayed snuggled up next to it for most of the day.

Later at the church, I put on my makeup and stepped into my dress. When I look back at the pictures, I looked so young and innocent. I had that feeling in the pit of my stomach all day long. Just nerves, you know? The six bridesmaids in their long-sleeved red velvet dresses with the lace insets had already walked down the aisle. There were candles glowing at the end of every pew. Candleabras on either side of the wedding party created eerie—I mean, romantic— shadows across the groom's face as he waited for me under the huge copper cross hanging from the steeple. My dad had already pulled my hand over his arm with a pat. He looked down at me. I must have looked terrified because he said, "You know, you don't have to do this. We can turn right around and walk down the staircase out of this church." The photographer caught the moment as my tears created black mascara rings under my eyes. I shook my head, "No," and my father reached over to wipe my tears away. The song I'd been waiting to hear my whole life began, and we walked down the aisle.

Sometimes it's confusing to decipher what our guts are saying. I wish I would have listened more intently, with integrity. I wish I would have asked my child-self whether it was time to run. She is so smart. When in doubt, run. Don't worry whether you will look stupid or uncool or absolutely nuts. Just run.

Did You Know / Necessary Facts

Intuition—Our Safe, Secret Subconscious

Intuition is:

- A feeling that something is going to be good or bad.

- The result of all of our accumulated experiences hanging out in our subconscious.

- Our subconscious drawing conclusions that we may not be able to see.

- Random moments, memories and values that can influence split-second decisions.

- When our subconscious takes over because there's no time for our practical mind to process pros and cons of a situation.

Examples of Intuition:

- A sense that someone is looking at us.

- A sense that a person is unsafe.

- A sense of knowing that we should or should not do something or should or should not go somewhere.

- A sensation of tightness in the neck or shoulders.

- A change in our breathing or heart rate.

- A feeling in our gut.

The two operating systems in the brain that help us negotiate decisions:

System #1—Feeling and Intuition ➜ Thinking Fast*

- quick, instinctual, effortless

- draws on patterns collected by our experience

- subconscious process used when we need to make a quick decision about whether something is real/fake, good/bad, right/wrong

System #2—Logic and Reason ➜ Thinking Slowly*

- more analytical and deliberate

- conscious thought process (like a list of pros and cons)

*NOTE: System #1 knows the right answer long before System #2

Why Should We Listen to Our Intuition?

- It can keep us safe.

- It is often faster and more correct than our intellect.

- Intuition helps us draw on past experiences that hold lessons and clues.

- We can learn "reset" mode after mistakes instead of "repeat" mode.

- Our body, mind and intuition can learn to work together for our best interest.

Tips to Help Your Intuition Keep You Safe

- Trust your gut feelings. There are millions of neurons in your stomach. Have you ever felt "sick to your stomach" before a big test or decision?

- Pay attention to your body's responses. Do you have butterflies, goosebumps, shivers down the spine, a fast heartbeat?

- Pay attention to surroundings and strangers.

- Get rid of negative friends/people when you can. If you take on negative feelings, you may not recognize what your intuition is telling you. For example, it's hard to make a good decision when you're angry.

- Surround yourself with positive people.

- Find quiet times to meditate, stretch, or do yoga.

- Opt out when your intuition is giving you a bad feeling. Have a list of excuses ready: I don't feel well. My mom said I couldn't. My teacher said she'd fail me if I don't turn my paper in tomorrow. I'm on restriction.

- Decide ahead of time what your personal boundaries are. These limits protect us and let others know what is acceptable and not acceptable to us (see **Chapter 22**).

Your Story

I interviewed a sixteen-year-old girl named Lisa. She remembered a time when she was fourteen. Her older brother was eighteen and often had his friends over. One day her brother's friend asked her if she wanted to meet him at a certain neighborhood location and go somewhere with him. She felt flattered that an older guy would want to hang out with her. The next day, she went to the street where she was supposed to meet him and saw him in the distance coming toward her. A feeling came over her that something was not right, and before she could even think, her body took off running in the opposite direction. Looking back on it, she could see that it was unusual for an eighteen-year-old guy to be interested in a fourteen-year-old. He probably only wanted one thing: something she didn't want to give him. Her intuition took care of her without her having to put any thought into the decision.

Another girl named Reiko is eighteen years old and told me about a party she went to with her girlfriend, Sora. The girls were in San Diego on a student exchange program from another country and had been living with their host families for one month when I interviewed Reiko. They were invited by some other friends in their program, but they did not know the people hosting the party. Both girls wanted to meet American teens, and were not concerned that they didn't know everyone.

They arrived at the house party in a neighborhood near SDSU where they attended classes. It was about 8:45 p.m. Reiko was home by 11 p.m. and Sora did not return home until 10 a.m. the next morning.

"There were about five people we knew and everyone else we didn't know. Everyone was friendly. Snacks, brownies, and lots of alcohol were out on the table. There were four guys hosting the party. They were in their late twenties—one was twenty-seven, two were twenty-eight, and one was twenty-nine. They were encouraging everyone to eat the brownies. I found out they were pot brownies."

Reiko stopped to ask me a question. "Can you buy these brownies in a store?"

"Not really," I answered. "Usually they buy the marijuana and add it to the brownie batter."

Reiko continued.

"I didn't have a brownie, but Sora did. Everyone thought it was very funny. The hosts were encouraging everyone to drink shots. Over the next two hours, Sora had six shots and a brownie. They kept saying, 'Drink, drink, drink! Have another shot!' They asked me over and over, but I didn't want to drink in the United States because it's against our program rules. I was also afraid I would be breaking the law. At home, it's also against the law. I have had a little to drink at parties in my own country, but I didn't want to here in the U.S.

"Over the next two hours, I became more and more nervous and uncomfortable. I talked to people around the room—especially my own friends—but also to the hosts. That's how I found out their ages and that only one of them went to San Diego State."

Reiko paused again. "Is it usual for older guys who don't go to college to have parties with young people who do?"

I answered, "No. I think that's unusual."

"Sora was already drunk, and I was worried for her. I didn't know how that much alcohol and pot would affect her, but I also was worried that the program would find out what she did and send her home.

"I knew it was time for me to leave when I saw a young guy pass out on the floor. I had been watching the hosts almost forcing shots down him, yelling, 'Shot! Shot! Shot!' Sora and I had been dropped off by one of our host moms, and we were planning to stay together and share an Uber ride back to our houses. I went to Sora and said, 'I'm leaving now. I want you to come with me. That guy just passed out, and you've had a lot to drink already.' She said, 'No, I'm not leaving. I'm having a good time. I love all these people.' She was very drunk, and I tried to convince her to come with me, but she wouldn't. I felt scared for myself and for her, but I knew I needed to get out of there as quickly as possible.

"I called Sora when I got home, but she wouldn't answer. I called her all the next day, and there was no answer. I was so worried. I found out late the next day that she spent the night at the party house along with some other drunk people. She did not bring a purse so she had no money, no credit card, no address for her host family. Her cell phone was dead. Even when she was ready to go home the next morning, she couldn't do anything but start to walk, hoping she was going in the right direction. She wasn't paying attention to the route on the way to the party because she was on the phone talking to her friends. It took her two hours to finally arrive at her host family's house, even though the party house was only a five-minute drive away."

I asked Reiko whether the guys who lived in the party house tried to take advantage of Sora. She didn't think so, but wasn't sure.

What makes one teen able to connect with their intuition and recognize that something bad might happen, and one teen be completely unaware of danger? The obvious answer in this story is alcohol, of course, but why didn't Sora recognize anything odd *before* she got drunk? Four guys in their late twenties invited young students, mostly girls, from another country—who didn't have a good sense for the language or the customs—to a party at their home. Three of them didn't even go to SDSU. Together, they had enough alcohol to get everyone drunk, had purchased marijuana, and made marijuana brownies for students ten years younger than them. Reiko's intuition alarm went off immediately, and Sora's did not.

I don't have the answers to all of these questions, but I wonder, based on what we've learned so far, whether Sora's intuition was underdeveloped or she hadn't practiced using it enough. Maybe she didn't discuss her opportunities and experiences and mistakes and achievements with an adult who could help her negotiate those events. Maybe she didn't learn how to make good decisions and what to do when bad decisions were made. Maybe she didn't have adults who taught her values and morals and how to tell right from wrong. Maybe she didn't have adults who made her feel safe and loved.

What I Wish My Mama Would Have Told Me

I wish my mama would have told me that when I get that feeling in the pit of my stomach that tells me I shouldn't do something or that danger is imminent or that I made a really, really bad choice, to run like the wind. I wish she would have told me that my intuition can save my life. I believe that it saved my life at least two times when I was growing up.

I wish my mama would have told me that there would be countless other times when I was sixteen and seventeen and then eighteen when my instincts would try to save me. I wish she would have told me to pay attention to my own body and heart and soul. "When those nerves in your stomach try to tell you that something isn't right, even if there is a cute boy involved, pay attention. Sometimes our desire and need to be loved can outweigh our instincts. When your instincts tell you to turn tail and run, listen. Don't lose that sense, my sweet daughter."

Opportunities to Journal

* Describe a time when you had a feeling in your gut that something wasn't quite right. What happened? What did you do? What did you learn?
* Have you ever made a decision that you felt you couldn't get out of later? What did you do?

✻ When you listen carefully to your intuition, what message do you get about what is important now and in your future? Thinking about these choices ahead of time can help keep you safe.

✻ Describe a time when you were not in any danger, but you got a feeling to join a club or become part of a team or choose a new friend that turned out to be a positive experience. That's intuition too!

✻ Make a list of opt-out phrases you could use if your intuition tells you not to go somewhere, like "I'm on restriction."

Take-Aways

✻ Intuition comes from all of your lessons, experiences, family values and memories.

✻ Sometimes your intuition doesn't work because you haven't had anyone to help you understand your experiences, mistakes and memories or you haven't learned enough about morals and values.

✻ Sometimes your desire to be liked and accepted or to be seen as cool gets in the way of your intuition.

✻ Sometimes you ignore your intuition because you want what you want instead of what your intuition says is good for you.

✻ Your intuition knows the right answer long before your logic does. Your intuition can save your life.

✻ You can choose to opt out when your intuition is giving you a bad feeling. Have a list of excuses ready!

✻ You can decide ahead of time what your personal boundaries are. You get to decide what is acceptable and not acceptable to you.

✻ When in doubt, run! Just run!

Chapter 10

Choosing a Partner . . . or Not

Do you enjoy watching a good teen comedy? There's always a romance, right? There are funny scenes about jealous friends, like two girls fighting over one guy, or two guys fighting over one girl. There are struggles with parents and teachers, and struggles with the desire to become more intimate. But in the end, doesn't the romance always work out and solve everything? Movies, social media, our culture in general give us messages that often tell us that teen romance is the answer.

Is having just one boyfriend or girlfriend something you are looking forward to? Maybe you have already met a special person and are learning the joys and frustrations of being in a relationship. Some of the students I talked to don't want to be in a serious relationship during high school. They have chosen to focus on school and have many friends with whom they hang out, study, and go to school dances and activities. I, on the other hand, spent my junior and senior years of high school with just one boyfriend. I pretty much gave up my girlfriends, and my boyfriend became the most important person in my life—even before my precious self.

When I was in high school, I didn't know what a healthy relationship looked like. I didn't know how much I needed my girlfriends and my family. I didn't know anything except the romantic notions I had picked up from movies, books, magazines, and friends. I was influenced more by my heart than my head. I ignored any signs that my boyfriend would end up like his scary parents. I didn't spend one moment thinking about whether I even wanted a high school relationship. I didn't know what I would be looking for in a partner if I did want one.

My Story

Massive sideburns. I couldn't take my eyes off of them. I was enrolled in a biology class the summer before my senior year. As Mr. Engberg lectured on habitats, I was distracted by the tall muscular TA with the alluring blue eyes and sandy brown mutton chops who circled the room preparing labs for later in the day.

After several weeks of eyeing each other and pretending we weren't, I sensed Mark approach the desk where I stood dissecting a frog.

"Hey, I'm wondering if you'll go to a movie with me tomorrow night."

Mark acted like a perfect gentleman. He didn't even try to kiss me. While we snuggled at the drive-in, I stroked his thick, curly sideburns, and he held my small hand in his big, masculine senior hand. I loved his kind, sexy, and shy grin.

I decided one hot day after the summer school session ended to surprise Mark and ride my bicycle the three miles to his house. I didn't have my driver's permit yet, and Mark had his license but no car to drive. My heart beat more from nervousness than exertion as I pulled into his driveway, got off my bike, and found my way to the front door. I knocked against the awkward screen door, waited, and then knocked again.

When the door abruptly opened, I could see the outline of a tall woman with a frame that filled the screen, and an even taller person peering over her shoulder. She didn't open the screen door, but I could feel her eyes piercing through the tiny aluminum wire squares.

"Who are you?"

"I'm Mark's friend. I came to see him."

In a sickeningly sarcastic voice, she said, "Well, isn't that sweet?"

The outline behind her spoke. "Mom, please. She's my friend from biology class."

"Girls don't come over to boys' houses."

"She came all this way on her bike. Can I go out and talk to her for a few minutes?"

"No. She should have thought about her behavior before she came across town unannounced. If the bike got her here, it can take her back home."

I raced home on my bike, tires hot with revolutions. The wind fought with the tears running down my face. I abandoned my bike in my front yard and collapsed on my bed, feeling like I'd just escaped from the Wicked Witch of the West. I was Dorothy on my bicycle. Toto was missing, but Dorothy and I were definitely simpatico.

Well, you know, the fairy tale high school romance proceeded flawlessly after I made it past the offending witch. No worries. Mark met my parents, who were unsure about this guy with the massive sideburns. Mark's mother seemed to move past her first impression of me, and one evening we stopped by Mark's house on our way to get something to eat. I met his father and brothers for the first time. Mark's mom, dad, and two younger brothers were putting together a puzzle. I remember thinking to myself, "Whew, that's a good sign." I felt a little relief after our rocky start.

As I got closer, I saw that it was a Playboy puzzle of a naked woman. They were just putting the final pieces in, and the conversation sounded a little something like this:

"Well, her boobs are a little small, but they have a nice shape."

"More than a mouth full's a waste."

"Her butt would make me happy."

"Well, I like those curly little hairs on the other side."

"You ain't getting any girl who looks nearly this good!"

"We know what happens when *you* dream."

Mark's father looked at me and winked. His mother laughed and said to Mark, "We know why Nancy likes your sideburns." *Seriously, he told them I liked his sideburns? And what exactly were they implying?*

As our young relationship grew and we dated consistently, Mark's parents realized that I wasn't just a sexual fling—which I honestly think they would have preferred. A matriarchal society existed in their household, which was a different experience for me. At my house, dad coming home at the end of a workday meant that five women—his wife and four daughters—were there to wait on him. He entered his kingdom, kissed his wife at the kitchen stove, put on his slippers, switched on the TV, and read his paper while listening to the news. My father didn't expect any special attention; it was just given to him without question.

At Mark's house, the opposite was true. Even though Mark's dad worked all day, his mom was the one waited on. Sometimes she would cook, sometimes dad would cook, but always dad yelled at the kids when mom directed him to:

"Did you hear me ask Randy and John to set the table? Do you see them doing it?"

Dad would scream, "Listen to your mother before I cross this room and make you!"

"Babe, I need another glass of wine," and Dad would be at her side in seconds.

Later, she might not feel appreciated after the meal she had prepared:

"Am I just the cook in this house? Does anybody have anything to say to me?"

"Tell your mother how wonderful this meal was."

"I guess we're all going to just sit here and look at these dirty dishes all night."

"Goddammit, boys, get this table cleared off and get the dishes done."

According to Mark, these scenes were calm compared to what could actually happen on any given night. Behind my back, Mark's mom and dad openly ridiculed what they thought was my "perfect little home life," but wanted to make sure I saw a certain quality of life when I visited their home. The few times I saw glimpses of Mark's reality were when the boys were threatened with a beating—always with a smile towards me from those who threatened—or actually backhanded for saying or doing something inappropriate. If the boys started to argue with each other, they might throw a few punches with their parents looking on. Either mom or dad might make fun of them for swinging like a girl, or laugh when one got popped too hard. Once his mom said to Mark, "Oh, you're so mad. You're so tough. Come on. Hit me. I'll flatten you." His dad laughed and said, "She could do it too, you know." Looking back on it, Mark's dad was the buffer between Mark's mother and me. He often looked over at me and winked or justified her behaviors when she left the room. Somehow, I think he had lost himself many years before. It wasn't that I didn't like this family so different than my own. I was intrigued by them in a sick kind of way. I had the feeling they were on their best behavior for my benefit, but I really had no idea to what extremes this family might go. I found out soon enough.

Your Story

I talked to hundreds of girls ages thirteen to eighteen during the years I taught high school. I shared my boyfriend stories from high school, and they shared theirs. I can't think of one time when a girl said, "I met his parents. They are so awesome! I can't understand why he's a jerk sometimes." Most girls met the parents and said something like, "His father drank too much, and his mother screamed at him and was rude to me, but he is *so* great. He's working hard to be better than his parents." I get it. Most teen boys (and girls for that matter), even if they come from difficult home situations, are fighting *not* to be like their parents. It's the nature of being a teenager.

There are stories of brave, determined teens who succeed despite their parents' choices and circumstances. I applaud them. In the real-life stories of my students, though, the boyfriends who did not have strong role models at home did not know how to treat their girlfriends. They may have started out sweet and romantic in the beginning, but the stories of how they acted towards the girls after time passed were often scary and sad.

When I interviewed Alexa—a junior in high school focused on her GPA and multiple after-school activities—she had a solution for the pain that can come from trying to maintain a relationship in high school. Choose not to. She said, "I don't need a partner. I'm doing a lot. I'm goal-oriented. I don't want to limit myself. I want to be successful. Choosing a partner would take away from my goals. I would have to balance both of our lives and integrate them with my already busy life." Alexa realized something about herself that many teens (and adults) aren't able to see.

She said, "Teens may not have a good support system, so they look for that in a relationship. It's rare that high school students end up in a healthy long-term relationship. Most teen relationships don't work and aren't healthy. Most of what I see in high school is students going through many relationships and break-ups. I see their mistakes and what happens because of their mistakes, and I don't need that."

Alexa fills her life with many friends and family members. She goes to events like dances with groups, "usually about ten of us."

Alexa feels so strongly about *not* having a relationship because she watched her sister go through one high school relationship drama after the next and allow those relationships to define her. Her sister's last high school relationship kept her from her dream to join the Army because she didn't want to leave her boyfriend. The relationship didn't last anyway. During her next relationship, she did graduate from dental assistant school, but the relationship ended after two years. Finally, she reunited with a high school crush, and after three years he asked her to marry him. "Even then, my sister was afraid of the commitment and made a mistake with another man. This boyfriend was willing to work on the relationship and go to therapy. He said he wasn't going to let one mistake ruin their lives. He showed maturity. He helped her go to school, and she's currently working on her bachelor's degree."

Alexa said that she remembered all of these relationship dramas and wanted to avoid them when she was in high school. She gave me this list of why to say "no" to intimate high school relationships:

* I don't want to be held back.
* I don't want to give my time to a relationship.
* I think that teens make bad decisions when they are focused on being in a relationship.
* I watched my sister hop from relationship to relationship.
* I don't want to waste my potential on someone else.
* I can't afford to get distracted with a possibly unhealthy relationship.

When I talked to a sophomore named Patricia, she was embarrassed by how naïve she was when she was a freshman. She had her first serious boyfriend and thought everything was going well. She thought he would never leave her. She said, "If I would have been honest with myself, I would have realized two freshman teens don't end up together, but I was stupid. I didn't want it to be true that we might break up. I was optimistic that we would stay together."

She shared with me three signs that told her their young relationship was going to end: "1) When I texted him, he responded 'K.' To a teen, if someone you like sends you a 'K,' it feels like your whole world is crumbling down. 2) He avoided me. He didn't want to talk. Every time I tried to hug him or show affection towards him, he seemed uncomfortable. 3) He texted me, 'We need to talk later about something.'"

Patricia's boyfriend did not talk to her in person. He broke up with her over a text message. She said, "I felt like my heart shattered in a billion little pieces, and I was crying all night and the rest of the next day. It was a nightmare." Patricia said it took her about three weeks to get over the pain she felt. Her lesson? "I can't change the way someone else feels; every person makes his own decisions and has his own emotions."

In the end, both Alexa and Patricia came to the same conclusion: Having a high school relationship can make life more challenging, difficult, and dramatic. Alexa was stronger for her sister's mistakes, and Patricia had an improved sense for what she wanted in the remainder of her high school years.

Healthy Relationship Diagram

What Does a Healthy Relationship Look Like?

- Take care of yourself and have good self-esteem apart from your partner.
- Respect each other's individuality and separate activities.
- Express yourselves openly and honestly to each other without fear of consequences.
- Feel secure and comfortable and encourage other relationships.
- Take interest in each other's activities.

- Trust each other and be honest with each other.

- Have respect for sexual boundaries.

- Resolve conflict fairly (see Fair Fighting in **Chapter 19**).

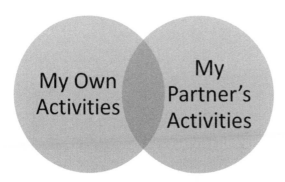

This Venn diagram represents a healthy relationship where two people have been together for a while, share lots of common interests, but maintain a separate space for themselves.

Left and right circles represent separate activities: Sports, family, friends, hobbies, alone time, jobs.

The center circle represents activities the couple does together: Dates, activities, sports, friends, etc.

If the relationship should break up, both are still grounded in their own life and activities. They may grieve the loss of the center circle, but will be able to move on with their life, counting on friends, family, and healthy diversions.

What Does an Unhealthy Relationship Look Like?

- Neglect yourself to put the other person first.

- Feel pressure to change who you are, or try to change the other person.

- Worry about disagreeing with the other person or pressuring the other person to agree with you.

- Feel pressure to quit activities you enjoy.

- Feel required to justify or explain where you go and whom you see.

- Do not make time to be together, or spend all of your time together.

- Have no common friends or lack of respect for each other's friends and family.

- Feel obligated or are forced to have sex; refuse safe sex methods.

- Arguments are not settled fairly and may involve yelling or physical violence.

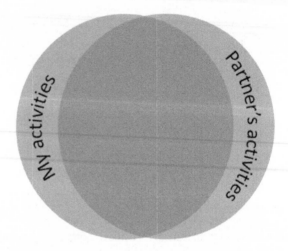

This Venn diagram represents an unhealthy relationship where there is not much "you" left on either side of the large circle. This relationship is stifling and could be abusive.

Left and right circles represent only minimal separate activities.

The two people only maintain a sliver of independence.

The center circle represents "together time."

In this relationship the two people count on the other person to fill their time and bring them fulfillment.

If the relationship should break up, the two individuals have lost most of themselves and are only left with a sliver of who they used to be. The grief is overwhelming and each person will have to try and replace the other as soon as possible to return to some semblance of normalcy.

What I Wish My Mama Would Have Told Me

I wish my mama would have told me to look at my friends' and boyfriend's or girlfriend's families and to notice what kind of home environment they had. And I wish she would have told me that, most of the time, we end up very much like the parents who raised us. I wish my mama would have told me that girls can't change boys, even if they like or love them very, very much. (There are exceptions.) It's the way we've been nurtured; it's the way we've seen the world work from the time we were babies. It's all we know.

I wish she would have told me to avoid choosing just one person during high school. I wish she would have told me that high school is about having lots and lots of interests and experiences and explorations. I wish she would have told me that I didn't need one guy to be my everything. And then I wish she would have explained to me the differences between a healthy relationship and an unhealthy relationship. I wish she would have helped me create a checklist for what I want in a future partner so that, when I was ready to choose, I would choose with confidence, boldness, and maturity.

Opportunities to Journal

* Think about a time when you met the family of a boy you know. Did you like the family? If you didn't like the family, did that change your view of whether you should become more involved with him?

* Ask your mom (or another adult) if they were ever interested in a boy, met his family, and were shocked by how different he was than his crazy/scary family. Did your mom think that she could "save" him from his family?

* Are you for or against serious high school relationships? Why or why not?

* Create your personal checklist for a healthy partner.

Take-Aways

* You can choose whether to have many friends with whom you hang out, study, and go to activities and dances. You can choose to have a more serious partner. Having a healthy definition of friends and partners can help you make the best decisions for you.

* Teens often end up with the same social mores and belief systems as their parents, but you have the choice to be aware of patterns so you can choose more wisely.

* Having many friends in high school—and observing how their families interact with them—can teach you a lot about what kind of person you want for a boyfriend.

* Most high school relationships do not last long and have many unhealthy components.

* In healthy relationships, both partners maintain busy, separate, fulfilling lives, and also share special activities together.

* In unhealthy relationships, partners spend the majority of their time together and only spend minimal time with their own friends and activities.

* Girls can't change boys, no matter how much they love them.

Chapter 11

LGBTQIA & Their Allies

The decision whether or not to have a romantic relationship in high school is a decision you will make, no matter your sexual/social orientation, but I want to spend some extra time talking about teens who identify as LGBTQIA. During your time in high school, you will hear many stories about people who are lesbian, gay, bisexual, transgender, queer, intersex, and asexual (LGBTQIA). You will have to decide which stories are hateful or untrue and which stories are loving and supportive.

If you identify as LGBTQIA, you have the same emotions and struggles deciding whether to have a steady partner in high school; however, you have a set of problems unique to your identification. You may have already experienced bullying, name-calling, homophobia, coming-out struggles, and self-hate. You may feel more judgment than your heterosexual friends when you are attracted to someone and are exploring those emotions. You may be wondering how you're going to figure out whether a gay community even exists at your school.

Whether you identify as LGBTQIA or not, you have probably used or heard someone else use "gay" as a derogatory term. When a teen identifying as "gay" hears the word used negatively, the impact is hurtful at best. The good news is that today there are organizations like Gay, Lesbian and Straight Education Network

(GLSEN) where LGBTQIA teens (and teens who care about them) can go for support and resources.

Let's take a closer look at labels, definitions, and information around the acronym LGBTQIA in the following chart.

Did You Know

LGBTQIA Definitions & Information

These labels are constantly changing and will continue to change based on the current generation and culture.

L—Lesbian	A woman who is emotionally, romantically, or sexually attracted to other women.
G—Gay	A man attracted emotionally, romantically, and/or sexually to other men. (Sometimes used as an umbrella term to include all LGBTQIA people.)
B—Bisexual	A person who is attracted to two sexes or genders, but not necessarily at the same time or equally.
T—Transgender	A person whose psychological self or gender identity differs from the social expectations for the physical sex they were born with. Think about the difference between someone's body (genitals, chromosomes, etc.) and someone's social gender (levels of masculinity and femininity).
Q—Queer/ Questioning (can be two "Qs")	Queer used to be a negative term towards anyone LGBTQIA, but now it's often used to mean anyone who identifies as LGBTQIA.
I—Intersex (aka non-binary or neutral)	Refers to someone whose anatomy or genetics at birth do not correspond to the typical expectations for either sex. It is different from transgender people, who are usually born either male or female in terms of anatomy but grow up to identify with the opposite gender.

A—Asexual/Allied	A person who does not feel sexual attraction or a desire for partnered sexuality. The "A" also indicates that allies are important, whether heterosexual or LGBTQIA.
LGBT or **LGBTQ**	Still often used to represent the LGBTQIA community.

Note: It's good to ask every person what culture or gender or LGBTQIA community with which they wish to identify. It is important for all of us, both heterosexual and LGBTQIA, to self-identify and for us to believe people when they do identify.

Resources: If you or anyone you know is struggling with any LGBTQIA issues, please check the **Resources** section in the back of the book.

My Story

Growing up, I didn't know there were folks who felt differently in their own skin. Who struggled to be female when they felt male, or vice versa. Who were attracted to the same sex. Who wanted to stay male or female, but wanted to dress like the opposite sex. Who enjoyed sexual relationships with both males and females. Who were born asexual. Who couldn't imagine another day of being the same person they saw in the mirror.

The following stories will use "homosexual" and "gay" since those are the terms with which I was familiar at the time. "Homosexual" is no longer a preferred term by the LGBTQIA community.

In high school, my best friend, Kerey, was in Drama class with a gay guy who either didn't know it yet or hadn't come to terms with it yet; he had a steady girlfriend. He would tell Kerey stories, I think, or maybe the stories were just dumped into the grapevine. Anyway, we knew that he and his girlfriend were having sex in the backseat of his car. Kerey said that somebody said that he said that he didn't really like "it" that much and neither did she. We just figured the dislike for sex probably had more to do with first-time jitters and the fear of being caught than an actual dislike for having sex with someone of the opposite sex. The backseat rendezvous ended in pregnancy, as they sometimes do, and the young couple were married and started their family. They were divorced within a couple of years, and the new dad's next relationship was with a man.

When my own sons were four, seven, and eleven, my brother-in-law got married. His wife's brother, Ethan, was gay, and at the time of the wedding was in his late twenties. He was in a committed relationship with his partner, Sam. Both Ethan and Sam gave kind and patient attention to the boys throughout the wedding weekend. My four-year-old was caught on film during the wedding day festivities in deep conversation with, or dancing with, or just watching his two new role models. The older boys asked if Sam was Ethan's boyfriend, but any negative stories they may have heard in school were quickly overshadowed by the mere fact that Ethan and Sam were amazing role models.

Over the next several years, we spent Thanksgiving with my brother-in-law, his wife, eventually their children, and Ethan and Sam. Ethan was the event planner for the weekend following Thanksgiving. We experienced bonfires on the beach, theater excursions, and boardgames. Ethan always had wonderful activities planned for my sons and later for his niece and nephew. One trip, as the boys all rolled out sleeping bags in the living room, Ethan took me aside and asked if he could tell my oldest son, who was probably fifteen at the time, about AIDS (Autoimmune Acquired Deficiency Syndrome) and birth control. AIDS had just recently come to the forefront on the news as a disease that often affected the gay community. I said I would be honored. I was thankful Ethan was a healthy, safe, gay man, willing to honestly inform my sons.

Ethan gave my sons the gift and the truth of himself. He embraced his sexuality and his family embraced him. It followed that he has the strength and love to be a positive role model for other young men. As a result, I never had to directly teach my sons to respect those who are homosexual, because they grew up respecting

Ethan, who happened to be homosexual. When you love someone, and another person speaks negatively about who they are—even if the negativity isn't directed toward your loved one—natural defenses go to work to support him or her at all costs. My two older boys probably had heard stereotypes about homosexuality, but the stereotypes were pretty quickly replaced with loving reality. My youngest son ended up traveling with a Broadway musical for several years in his young adulthood. The performing arts field is one safe haven of acceptance for gay people, and for my son the environment was a natural, exciting, creative place to live. He never had any stereotypes about gayness, and was shocked the first time he heard a negative comment about "homos" or being "gay." He can't even begin to understand the ignorance of those who do not accept people who are gay.

Your Story

It's difficult to be a teen under any circumstances. There are so many emotions and hormones and insecurities. But teens who identify as LGBTQIA have a set of problems unique to their identification. For example, all teens have pressure from parents regarding relationships, but LGBTQIA teens often have to deal with parents who may think they're just going through a "phase," and that their feelings aren't legitimate.

All teens find it confusing to be attracted to someone in high school. Does he like me? Should I ask her out? In heterosexual relationships, the way to find out who you like and who likes you is a little easier. You can flirt a little. You can mess around, hold hands, sit on someone's lap, maybe even kiss. If you identify as LGBTQIA, you may have to deal with homophobia, name-calling, bullying, and strong emotions and words if your attraction is not met with like feelings. (And how does one know for sure that another high school student is or is *not* LGBTQIA anyway?)

One teen guy who identifies as gay said, "If I was attracted to a guy, there was no way to know whether he felt the same way about me; odds are, most of the time he didn't. It was scary and embarrassing, and definitely not cool to ask a guy if he was gay." As a teen who identifies as LGBTQIA, you may feel that there is no safe place to go to meet other teens who might feel the same way you do. Looking for relationships with other LGBTQIA teens can end up putting you in potentially dangerous situations with older men and women met online or in other settings that are not normal teen hangouts.

I had the honor of interviewing one of my past high school students, now twenty-five, who shared with me her struggle from a young age to understand her emotions around her sexuality. As far back as elementary school, Adrian can remember liking girls. Her mother had even asked her in the sixth grade if she was gay, to which Adrian gave an emphatic, "No!" She remembers feeling bullied in elementary school. She said, "I was a tall, big, black nerd. I got accused of being white-washed because I didn't talk in the black slang of our neighborhood. I also watched how others treated gay kids."

In middle school, one of her gay friends asked her to go out. Adrian said about the young crush, "We went out for about a week. I felt butterflies. She forced me to admit that I liked her a lot. She had already come out to her friends, and she pressured me to come out too. I told her, 'You're going to be the first and last girl I ever go out with.'"

Adrian didn't want to go to hell. Everyone in her Pentecostal church knew that being gay was bad. She kept these feelings that she was not supposed to have stuffed deep inside of her.

As a high school freshman, she had lots of friends, but her father didn't allow her to date, so she didn't have to deal too much with questions of sexuality. Adrian said, "I wore a mask. I was the crazy, loud one. I wasn't comfortable in my skin yet. I was still hiding from who I was." After she turned sixteen and her father told her she was old enough to date, a popular guy on the football team asked her out. On their date, they held hands, and he asked to kiss her. Adrian said of the experience, "I felt absolutely nothing, and after one week I came out to him. I said, 'You're a really nice guy, but I like girls. I'm just not ready to talk about it yet.' He was cool and didn't tell anyone. I knew then, gloves off; I'm going to be who I am."

A month later Adrian came out to her friends. Most were very accepting. A common phrase she heard from some girls was, "It's fine, but just don't try anything with me." Adrian said she was filled with fear and asked herself, "What will my parents say? What will the world say?" Adrian's father accepted no excuses when it came to his daughters becoming all they could be. He encouraged competition, extracurricular activities, and high academic scores. Adrian talked about coming out to her parents:

"My mom was fine with me being lesbian. She said she had always known. When I told my father, I think I burst his bubble. He didn't know black people could be gay. It was a little hard for him when I started presenting as more masculine. I was forbidden to watch any gay sitcoms, YouTube, or any show talking about being gay. There are certain things my dad was not okay with. He was not okay with men dressing like women. He was not okay with effeminate guys. So maybe it was good that I was a girl dressing more masculine rather than the other way around. When I wanted to date a girl for the first time, my dad said, 'Don't date your sister's friends.'"

In Adrian's personal journey with her sexuality, she became interested in working out and getting healthy. She became a vegan and joined a school dance team. She was comfortable dressing more masculine, but she never felt comfortable calling herself "lesbian." She was okay with the term "stud," maybe because she had older cousins who presented as masculine and called themselves "studs."

She said, "It was helpful that I had family who looked like me. My friends and family were okay with having family members who identified as 'stud.'"

I asked Adrian if it was difficult for her to explore her interest in girls in the high school setting. She said she thought it was much harder for guys to be gay than for girls. "Girls are already more touchy-feely. No one looks down on girls if they hug each other or walk arm in arm or even sit on each other's laps. It's also okay for girls to be tomboys. There is more freedom for a girl to act any way she wants. It's okay for girls to be questioning their sexuality. It's even seen by some men as sexy for girls to be attracted to girls."

Adrian talked about the influence of film and TV on teen girls while she was in high school. She said that when Katie Perry came out with the song "I Kissed a Girl," it was actually bad for girls identifying as lesbian.

"I never liked it that some girls would act as if they were interested in me, but were really playing. Girls would kiss each other as a lark."

During her senior year in high school, Adrian describes a time of self-hate. She had never really identified as lesbian, but wasn't clear on whether she was a transsexual. She made a decision: "I can't change what God gave me. I'll take care of my lesbian body." After high school, Adrian couldn't get past the fact that something important was missing for her. When she was twenty-two, she made the decision that was right for her: She began transitioning into a male body.

I reconnected with Adrian seven years after high school, three years after his journey of transition began. His beard, his muscular chest and arms, did not change his beautiful eyes and beautiful heart. He was the same Adrian I had come to know and love in our high school days together.

Until we have high school clubs, support groups, and activities for *all* teens who are LGBTQIA in *all* high schools around the country, we are putting our teens in danger of going out into the world—possibly in unsafe scenarios—to explore relationships. Teens who are heterosexual have more opportunities to explore romance in high school through innocent gestures like holding hands, flirting, sitting on someone's lap, reaching out to touch someone they like, innocent kissing, openly hanging out, or going out with someone they are attracted to. Teens who are LGBTQIA may be bullied or ridiculed or worse if they attempt any of the same behaviors with a person of the same sex (or any other LGBTQIA scenario). High school programs like National Day of Silence sponsored by the Gay, Lesbian and Straight Education Network (GLSEN) are beginning to make a difference.

GLSEN's (Gay, Lesbian and Straight Education Network) NATIONAL DAY OF SILENCE

The National Day of Silence is a student-led national event where folks take a vow of silence to highlight the silencing and erasure of LGBTQIA people in schools all over the United States.

Many students and teachers at Hoover High School where I taught participated in this event yearly in April. We began our day in silence from the moment we arrived at school, and continued until the end of the school day. Teachers had to figure out a way to teach their classes without saying a word and students had to communicate with those teachers and students who were not participating in the day . . . and embody enough spirit of rebellion to fight for those without a voice.

For example, in my classroom, students arrived to see a message on the board that said, "Welcome to Day of Silence. Please take out your journals and take notes or respond to the videos playing on the screen." I played several videos on the struggles of teens who identify as LGBTQIA: being bullied, coming out, reactions of family and friends, suicide attempts and death. After the videos, I asked the students to respond by writing their reactions/perspectives about teens who identified as LGBTQIA. Here are some of the responses.

These quotes are from students who may not agree with homosexuality, but don't judge or disrespect:

"I don't care about the sexuality preference of people. On the other hand, I don't support it either. I don't care or judge if a person is gay because I believe that everyone should be free to live their lives just the way they want to and not be oppressed by it. What I do care about is the abuse, harassment, and hatred being thrown at gay people throughout the nation. People should live their life the way they want to live it, and let others be."

"I think men are made for women, and women for men. This does not mean I have the right to bully or disrespect people who disagree with me. Being gay is a way of loving someone of your own sex, not a lifestyle/fashion statement that we should promote. People should not become gay just because others are gay."

This quote was written by a student who believes people should mind their own business:

"My opinion on this issue is simple. If there are people who oppose the whole gay thing, why don't they just mind their own business and shut up about it? These haters should really get a life. If I don't like someone, I don't go out into the streets and start talking bad about them. Instead, I just pay as little attention to them as possible. The problem is people don't know how to mind their own business and respect other people's private lives. I mean, it's not like gays, lesbians, transgenders, etc. are trying to take over the world or anything."

This quote was written by a student who is gay:

"My opinion about this situation is that people should appreciate homosexuality because everyone is the same. We are all humans and even though we prefer same sex orientation does not mean that people should hate us. I'm Gay and Proud 2 Be One!"

This quote was written by a student who believes that God doesn't want us to be gay, but he loves us anyway:

"I am opposed to harassment and bullying towards homosexuals, lesbians, and transgenders. We as humans have no right to judge anyone, especially not mistreat them because it says in the Bible, Romans 2:1 that those who judge are just condemning themselves. I am also not saying I support gays, lesbians, and transgenders. I don't support them because God had a purpose when he created a man and a woman. God doesn't hate them because he is loving and merciful all the time. God loves homosexuals, lesbians and transgenders!! He is loving and he does not hate anyone!!"

This quote was written by a student who believes that it's ignorant to judge others:

"I am a Sudanese Christian who supports gays. Oh, and did I mention I am a woman. Based on all these facts, who am I to judge another human being based on his or her sexuality? I will not let my ignorance get the best of me and repeat history's oppressive, racist, destructive actions. The only thing that separates me from a gay is our sexuality. We still both have the same emotions, we both cry, we both laugh. Being straight doesn't make me superior to them, and being gay doesn't make them any less of a person. In my opinion, it actually makes you more of a person because you're able to accept you for you and not what society wants you to be. Look in the mirror and check your appearance before you decide to physically or verbally abuse someone else because you feel like what they're doing is wrong. Who are we to pick what's right or wrong? If you try to use the religious excuse, you are a hypocrite. The Bible teaches us to love equally and to judge no man. So why do we tend to continuously put up with wrong doings and mistreatment?"

Not one student, even those that wrote about why being LGBTQIA is wrong, said bullying or harassment was okay. And not one said that God did not love every LGBTQIA. Preach it, teens!!

What I Wish My Mama Would Have Told Me

I wish my mama would have told me that I would hear many stories about people who are lesbian, gay, bisexual, transgender, queer, intersex, asexual, or any other category we might learn about in the future. What my teen students taught me (and what my sweet mama didn't know) was that it doesn't matter whether being LGBTQIA comes naturally with birth, like being pronounced a girl or a boy. It doesn't matter whether it's something picked up in the schoolyard like a cold or chicken pox. It doesn't matter what religious institutions say about LGBTQIA individuals. None of it matters. When I say "it doesn't matter," I don't mean that all of these scenarios aren't difficult and charged with emotion for both the teen who identifies as LGBTQIA and her family. I just mean that love is what truly matters. The rest can be figured out.

I wish she would have told me to focus on the fact that the person who has decided for him or herself that he/she is LGBTQIA may be the next-door neighbor I've loved my entire life, my niece or nephew I've loved my entire life, or my son or daughter I've loved my entire life. I wish she would have told me that love for another human being should never be dependent upon his or her sexual orientation. That the *idea* of lovingly accepting people who are LGBTQIA doesn't require that we love every LGBTQIA we meet, just like we don't have to love every random person we've ever met. I wish she would have said, "There are bad people in the world. You still get to dislike them strongly or even hate them if you so choose. But have good reason. Please don't let your reason be that he or she is a person who identifies as LGBTQIA."

Finally, I wish my mama would have told me, "Honey, if you

think you are LGBTQIA or know for sure that you are LGBTQIA, nothing changes for me. You are still the little girl I held in my arms on the day that you came into my life. This is your life. I love you."

I wish she would have told me to recognize the difficult journey those who identify as LGBTQIA experience. There is always fear and insecurity that comes from facing a reluctant society on any front that is worth facing, but LGBTQIA often have to face their own family and loved ones who may not understand or accept what they are going through. I wish she would have told me to recognize the bravery it takes for LGBTQIA folks to accept themselves and find a voice to express who they truly are.

Opportunities to Journal

* Have you ever experienced any of the emotions in this chapter, either because you're LGBTQIA or because you are an ally of someone who is?

* If you had been in my class, what would you have written about LGBTQIA?

* What would you like to talk about with your parent or another important person?

* Have you ever been bullied or seen someone bullied because of his/her sexual/social orientation? If so, explain what happened and how you felt about it.

* Have you ever thought of reaching out to an organization for community or information? Conduct your own search and make a list of organizations in your community.

Take-Aways

* LGBTQIA stands for lesbian, gay, bisexual, transgender, queer/questioning, intersex, asexual/allied. The terms by which individuals identify are constantly changing. It's important to be sensitive to the way each individual self-identifies.

* LGBTQIA teens have a more difficult time exploring their sexuality than heterosexual teens because of bullying, name-calling, homophobia, coming-out struggles, and self-hate.

* Teens need to feel safe and have extracurricular activities that support who they are so they don't seek unsafe relationships with older adults.

* There are many supportive organizations for LGBTQIA teens like GLSEN (Gay, Lesbian & Straight Education Network); It Gets Better Project; Crisis Lines; Trans Lifeline, National Runaway Safeline; and The Trevor Project (see **Resources** for contact information).

Chapter 12

Stages of Intimacy

Are you in a relationship with someone you've been adoring for a while? Do you dream of being intimate with a special person? What do you think of when you hear the word intimacy? In my sixteen-year-old brain, intimacy translated to one question: How far am I going to go with my boyfriend? Intimacy is more complicated, though.

I know now that sex is an important part of an intimate relationship, but I can have intimate relationships without sex being a factor at all. I know now that sex does not prove my love to anyone. I know now that we all long for intimacy and physical contact, but physical contact alone is not intimacy. I know now that the highest form of intimacy is emotional and spiritual, and that it exists inside of me.

But let's address the fact that sex is an important part of intimacy. You may be ready to move into sexual intimacy with your partner or have already. That may be the perfect decision for you. Later in the chapter, we'll go over some questions to ask yourself about when and why you want to have sex, whether you know about and are ready to openly discuss facts about pregnancy, birth control, and STDs with your partner, and whether you are emotionally ready to fully give your consent on your own terms (see Did You Know Chart: The Four "I"s of Intimacy).

My Story

The first many times Mark and I kissed, I was timid and he was patient. I had never French kissed before, and I could tell he wanted to because I could kind of feel his tongue muscle searching for mine. I just didn't know what to do. So embarrassed. When I finally decided I was going to surprise him and go for it, the consequence was mortifying. I'm not blaming my mom. I know moms don't teach you how to French kiss. If anything, they want to sew your lips shut. But a little help would have been nice. I thrust my tongue in there like I was trying to grab the brass ring on the merry-go-round (Google it). I nearly did both of our tongues some major damage. He knew what was in it for him, so he said something smooth like, "Slow down, girl. Take it easy." I confessed that I had never tried French kissing before. No shock there. So my sweet, sexy new boyfriend taught me how to French kiss. Then he taught me other things.

The summer ended and I started my junior year with a boyfriend. Mark drove me to school. We necked in the car a bit before school started, making my popularity go up significantly with those who passed by Mark's blue bomb. He walked me to my classes, kissed me good-bye, and was right there to pick me up at the end of class. We did homework together. He turned in more assignments his senior year than he probably turned in his entire high school career because I was a good student and wasn't willing to give that up.

My sweet Mark was working on being born again at a local fundamentalist church. The poor guy, trapped in a demented household with deranged parents, was merely trying to listen to the angels circling like a halo around his head. On our journey to stay as far away as possible from hell—considering all the kissing we were doing—we went to youth group, sang the inspirational hymns, and went to concerts of Christian singers. Of course, we struggled with the usual problems of high school relationships: How much kissing? How much touching? Was God watching?

Right here at this juncture, I would have liked to know that kissing is just fine. But serious kissing? Tongue-to-tongue, hot, passionate, sweaty, heart-beating-out-of-your chest kissing is rarely going to stop there. Unless. You. Have. Nerves. Of. Steel. I would have wanted to know that God doesn't hate me because I'm kissing my boyfriend in the front seat of his new green Datsun with the black stripe. I'm not disappointing him or my parents. I'm not a bad person because I want to go further than kissing. It's just the nature of the beast. Our bodies are wired that way. Unfortunately, often the arguments and facts teenagers are given for not having sex are about religion and pregnancy. I'm not discounting these arguments, but these arguments are not what would have changed my mind.

The whole religion argument made me feel super guilty every time we kissed, and probably put me through more teenage trauma and drama than I needed. Because we kissed anyway. It's what teenagers do. The more we kissed, the more I cried. I thought I was a sinner. I tried to stop. My boyfriend tried to stop. We continued to go to youth group. I thought God hated me and that my parents would be so *disappointed* in me. So I couldn't talk to anyone.

Mark would come over in his Farrell's Ice Cream Parlour black slacks and white shirt, freshly showered, on his way to work. Early on, we would snuggle on the love seat in the sitting room by the front door until time for him to leave. We couldn't make out since my mom was usually in the kitchen six feet behind us, but Mark would take my hand and bring it to the lump in his slick black slacks, wordlessly asking me to stroke that which I had not yet seen. It wiggled and throbbed, and I could not visualize what was happening; it felt like some kind of wormy creature growing under my touch. There was always a convenient afghan on the love seat, and we were always just a little bit cold.

The make-out sessions in the car got more intense until I finally saw the creature make its way outside Mark's jeans, reaching its full girth. He was discovering my body as well, and we had rounded to third base (see Did You Know chart).

The "having sex" argument wasn't even on the table. The questions in my head cycled as wildly as a tornado. Some of the questions were for my teenage self. Some were for any adult that might be questioning my relationship or my choices. But I didn't have the nerve to actually ask anyone for help.

Why are folks even talking about pregnancy? It's out of the question. I am NEVER going to have sex before I'm married.

How could you even suspect that I would? You don't trust me. You don't love me.

What kind of parent or church counselor or minister or sex-ed teacher are you?

I wasn't *really* talking to anyone but myself . . . and myself wasn't helping at all. If I had directed a conversation outside my head to a parent or another adult, I might have talked about Playboy puzzle night, the smell of alcohol at Mark's house, the holes in the walls. Then I might have shared about Mark's temper, and that we had passed second base, and the third base coach had motioned us to make a break for home more than once. I hadn't complied yet, but I was getting scared. Maybe talking would have kept me from marrying Mark at eighteen.

Did You Know / Fun Facts

> Above, I referred to "the bases" and "a homerun." Gianna, the teen I interview below, said she knew those terms, but no one really used them anymore. She said teens usually just talk about what "phase" of the relationship they're in. I thought it would be fun to compare the "phases" of today to the "bases" of the '70s.

Today's Phases	**"Old School" Bases**
	No boyfriend/girlfriend distinction:
Phase 1: Dating <ul><li>Hugging</li><li>Hand holding</li></ul>	No equivalent base
Boyfriend/girlfriend: **Phase 2:** <ul><li>Kissing a. Closed-mouth kissing b. Open-mouth kissing</li></ul>	**First Base:** Kissing, including open mouth or French kissing with tongue
Phase 3: <ul><li>Caressing and touching over clothes</li></ul>	**Second Base:** Touching and fondling above the waist, including chest, breasts, nipples. Shirts/tops off or on.
Phase 4: <ul><li>More intimacy a. Clothes come off b. Genital touching c. Oral sex</li></ul>	**Third Base:** Touching or orally stimulating below the waist, including vagina, clitoris, penis or testicles.
Phase 5: Intercourse	**Homerun:** Intercourse

"a, b, c" designations mean that the phase progresses; all these things don't happen on the same date. Later in **Your Story**, teens and experts talk about *six stages* that come before the first date!

Your Story

I'll be honest. I thought that when I researched current studies about teens and intimacy and then talked to teens face to face, I would find out that things move faster today than they did in the '70s. And maybe sometimes they do move quickly, and the teens have considered all of the intimacy questions and are ready. I searched "stages of high school dating" and checked out the first ten hits to find out how ideas may have changed since the '70s. Sources were everything from high school newspaper articles to well-known sites like *Huffington Post*. I found that the labels we put on stages of intimacy have changed—mostly due to the internet—but how fast 21st century teens get through the stages may actually be slower than teens in the '70s. I compiled my findings—with help from my high school consultant, sophomore Gianna—into six stages of high school dating:

Mutual friends: My friend asks his friend if he's interested in me. If he says yes, then his friend tells my friend who tells me. Then we hook up. (I remember this one, but now a lot of the work can be done with texting or messaging.)

Photo Op: If I don't go to the same school or I meet someone online, maybe we send each other pictures or selfies. If we like the looks of each other, we might friend each other, add each other, or text.

Awkward Stage: If we do go to the same school, but we haven't talked face to face, now we have to make the scary step to say "hi" in the halls. Mutual friends might do their thing again and force us into a face-to-face.

We're Talking: When people ask if we're together, we say, "No, we're just talking." We text back and forth during the day and maybe meet at Starbucks.

We're a Thing: Now we can say we're together because we hang out and we've told each other we like each other. We go to movies, restaurants, and school functions together. This stage could last a long time.

We're Dating: This stage makes our relationship official. The boy has usually asked the girl to officially be his girlfriend. When we're boyfriend/girlfriend, we make it known to our friends and go places with each other and our friends, but as a couple.

Later I researched major studies from well-known organizations like Centers for Disease Control and Prevention (CDC), Planned Parenthood, and Pew Research Center. Most of these studies were conducted using surveys of teens between the ages of thirteen and nineteen. What the numbers are saying is that the percentage of teens having some dating or romantic experiences has gone down significantly since I was a teen. Sixty-four percent of those surveyed in 2015 had never been in a romantic relationship, and out of the remaining teens surveyed, only fourteen percent had at least one serious relationship. Out of that fourteen percent, two-thirds were *not* sexually active.

The bottom line in all of the studies I read? Teens of today may be more responsible than the teens of past decades. From the time I was a teen—specifically in the late '70s—the desire to get a driver's license is down and the time students spend with their parents is up. Using alcohol is down by almost half for tenth graders. The number of high school students dating is down. The number of high school students having sex is down significantly. It's important to notice that what teens say on their private surveys is not always reflected in the media. Unfortunately, teens are pressured every day to act, dress, and behave far older than they are. Sometimes this pressure comes from outside sources like movies, television, and social media, but sometimes it comes from teens themselves. I love that the teens I interviewed were aware of the pressures, were aware of their social media personas, and when they made mistakes, they knew they could start over.

What Do You Want to Know about Intimacy?

I'm going to list some questions I had for the girls I interviewed and some general answers. I found that the topic of intimacy and how far girls have gone romantically was easier for girls to answer in general terms. I understand that no one wanted to out themselves or their friends.

NANCY: *How long does a typical couple in high school date?*

GIRLS: **About six months.**

NANCY: *How far do couples get in terms of how intimate they are in six months?*

GIRLS: **Most stay in the making-out phase. Some go further, but a lot of girls don't want to do more because they know that the relationship probably isn't going to last long.**

NANCY: *What is your definition of "intimate"?*

GIRLS: **Being really close to a guy or girl and sharing everything with them.**

Loving someone and feeling completely comfortable with that person.

Showing that you love and care for someone through your actions (holding hands, kissing, showing your love).

NANCY: *Is being in a serious relationship with a partner important to you?*

GIRLS (most said things like): **Not really. I'm not in any hurry to have all the problems that come with a serious relationship. I have a lot of friends and a lot of interests. I'm involved in sports and that's my focus. Going to college and being able to help my family in the future comes first.**

(One girl said) **I was in a serious relationship once and felt pressured to move too quickly. I went further then I wanted to** go. It's awkward now when I see him, and neither of us was ready. I'm lucky that I didn't get pregnant because my whole life would have changed.

Then just to mix it up, I asked them if they had any questions for me. Here's what we came up with:

GIRLS: **When did you know you were ready to have sex?**

NANCY: *When I had sex with my boyfriend, it was in high school. I was not ready to have sex. We were having arguments about it, and I felt pressured to "save his manhood." I know now that I should have waited for a partner who didn't get angry or make me feel guilty when I said no. The next relationship I had many years later, I knew I was ready because the decision was 100% mine, and we had a relationship of mutual respect and trust.*

GIRLS: **Do you think a couple can be intimate without having sex? Is sex the most intimate thing in a relationship?**

NANCY: *I used to think sex was the most intimate step in a relationship. But when I think about it now, I know two things:*

1) *Sex is an act that can be done quickly without any kissing or affection of any kind. The partners don't have to talk, look at one another, or even like each other.*

2) *Sex can be part of an intimate relationship if first there have been intimate conversations about emotions, likes and dislikes in every aspect of life, a life together after high school, what they truly believe in. Sex, alone, is not intimate.*

GIRLS: **When you and your boyfriend started getting more serious, were you nervous that something might go wrong or that you might get pregnant?**

NANCY: *I was very nervous. That's one of the reasons we had so many fights about it. I know now that being nervous might have meant I wasn't ready, and that the decision was not my own. Being nervous is probably why sex is not good the first time for most girls. Girls need to be relaxed so that the body is aroused and can receive the guy without pain. My boyfriend and I had talked a lot about sex, but we never once talked about birth control or what would happen if I got pregnant. The first time I had sex, we did not use protection and it was not an enjoyable experience.*

GIRLS: **It's so obvious what an orgasm means for a guy, but what does being aroused, and then having an orgasm mean for a girl?**

NANCY: *Great question that isn't talked about enough, right? Being aroused is that feeling you get when you're kissing a partner and maybe doing a little more. Maybe you've also felt it when you masturbate. Your breathing gets faster and your heart beats faster. For a girl, there are usually contractions of the vaginal muscles, and an intense feeling of pleasure that can include the clitoris, vulva, and/or vagina.*

Let me add a word or two on masturbation. Masturbation is a normal, healthy way to get in touch with your own body. You can learn about your body and experiment with what brings you pleasure. Masturbation can be a way to relieve stress. It's actually good for a future pleasurable relationship because you will know what makes you feel good, and you can help your partner satisfy you.

GIRLS: **Isn't it better just to convince the boy to mess around and maybe have oral sex? Then there is no risk of getting pregnant?**

NANCY: *Yes, that could be better for sure, at least in terms of pregnancy. Again, for me, it's about whether you have a loving, open relationship where you're talking about all of these choices. It's all about what you want to do, not what you are doing for him because you want to stay in the relationship. Oral sex, to me, feels more intimate than sex in a lot of ways because it puts each of you in a vulnerable position where you are offering your body parts to another person in a way that can be more personal than intercourse.* (Note: See **Chapter 13** to learn more about STDs in relation to oral sex.)

Maybe you've done your intimacy work and have decided not to be sexually active right now. Maybe you've done your intimacy work and have decided that being sexually active with your current partner is the right choice for you. Maybe today you have had the opportunity to make some different decisions for yourself regarding a current relationship. Your personal bottom line? You get to decide what's best for you, and you get to change your mind any time you want.

Did You Know

	The Four "I"s of Intimacy
Ideals	▪ Is having sex the right choice for me at this time of my life?
	▪ Am I considering sex because I truly want to have sex with this person?
	▪ Am I on board with my heart, soul, and mind? Is this 100% my choice?
	▪ Would I be proud to share this info with anyone in my life (family, friends)?
Infatuation	▪ Am I infatuated with my partner? In love? Why do I want to do this? (If my answer is "Because he/she wants me to" or "he/she will love me more" or "my friends are doing it" and not because it is my own decision about my own body, maybe my answer is "No.")
	▪ Do I understand the emotional risks for me as a result of giving my body to someone else?
	▪ If I want this because it is my true desire and I want this

Itemized Facts	• Do I know about pregnancy, birth control and STDs?
	• Have I discussed protection and where to get it with my partner?
	• If the contraception doesn't work, have we discussed our options?
Interpretation	• Taking the first three "I's" into account, what is my interpretation of the facts, my emotions and my decision?
	• I can talk to a parent or other trusted adult if I need help making this decision.

stage of intimacy, then I fully consent on my own terms. (I can change my mind at any time.)

What I Wish My Mama Would Have Told Me

What I wish my mother would have told me is that high school relationships are not even about kissing or sex. They're about exploring who you are and what kind of person you want to spend the rest of your life with, or even if you want to spend the rest of your life with any person. I would have wanted my mother to say, "Hey, honey. I see the signs that you're getting pretty involved with Mark. I imagine you're in the hot, steamy kissing stage, huh?" Yes, I would have been mortified. But looking back on it, I would have been a little intrigued. If she had told me some of her own high school stories about dating and kissing and why and when it worked and why and when it didn't, I would have been blown away . . . in a good way.

And if she would have told me that she wasn't trying to talk me out of kissing, she would have had my attention. If she would have asked me, "Have you found it hard NOT to go from kissing to touching, and then wanting more?" I would have wondered if she'd been hiding out in the backseat of Mark's car. If she would have said, "That happened to me, too," and told me how guilty and scared and hypersexual she felt sometimes, I would have thought, "Thank God, I'm not the only one." THEN, if she would have told me that Mark is a super nice guy and probably kisses really well, but wouldn't it be nice to take some pressure off and go to dances and concerts and parties with lots of different people until you're sure you have the perfect guy? Well, I may have been relieved. Because I was under a lot of pressure. I might have curled my fingers in those sexy sideburns, taken one last, long, wet kiss, and . . . broken up with him.

Opportunities to Journal

* Reading about intimacy and some of the terms that describe sexuality and sex, what are you thinking about or what questions do you have?
* How far do you think girls should go in high school?
* What have you heard about being intimate with a guy/girl?
* What stories would you like to hear from your mom?

Take-Aways

* Sex is an important part of an intimate relationship, but you can have intimate relationships without sex being a factor at all. The highest form of intimacy is emotional and spiritual. It exists inside of you.
* You can ask yourself intimacy questions, like when and why you want to have sex, whether you know about and are ready to openly discuss facts about pregnancy, birth control, and STDs with your partner, and whether you are emotionally ready to fully give your consent on your own terms.
* Kissing can end up in a hot mess. You can be in charge of how much kissing you want. Or whether you want any at all.
* There are usually phases or stages you go through as you become more intimate with a partner. Statistics show that teens of today may be more responsible with many decisions than the teens of

past decades.

* All those words like petting, fondling, oral stimulation, vagina, clitoris, penis, testicles, intercourse, consent, communication with a partner? Those words are important. Use reliable sources so that you know what they are and what they mean.

* High school relationships don't have to be about kissing or sex. They can be about exploring who you are and what kind of person you want to spend the rest of your life with, or even if you want to spend the rest of your life with any person.

* Try to make decisions based on your personal power. If you feel pressured, it's okay to say adios. If you make mistakes, you can start over.

Chapter 13

Sex: The Good, the Bad & the Ugly

Not to be a downer, but everything about sex is not good. Don't get me wrong; there's a lot that is good about sex. There really is. I just wish I hadn't had sex in high school in the places I did for the reasons I did. I hope that when you have sex for the first time it is not in the backseat of a small Datsun because the guy you think you love manipulated you. The good about sex comes in a long-term committed relationship with a partner who has taken the time to know everything about you and respects you enough to protect you and understand that your emotions are more important than the physical act.

We have to talk about the bad and the ugly, though, because it's the right thing to do. We need to be aware of the ways girls can be used as objects. We need to know that it's difficult to involve ourselves in the physical act without attaching emotion. We need to know that sex without full consent is rape. We need to know that when we don't have a safe, protected sexual experience, we may end up pregnant or with any number of sexually transmitted diseases (STDs). We'll talk in this chapter about the good, the bad, and the ugly of having sex.

Note: STDs are also known as sexually transmitted infections (STIs). Technically you can have an infection without having a disease, but in this section I will use STD to mean either.

My Story

So why and when did I have sex that first time? Contrary to what you might be thinking, the reason he scored a *homerun* that night was not because we were visiting all the *bases* and were caught up in the moment. We were having a discussion, in fact—one more time—about why we would or would not "go all the way."

We were making out in his car, parked in the darkest lot of the movie theater. Our making-out sessions had to be in the movie theater parking lot because I had told my parents we were going to a movie, and I didn't feel like I was lying if I truly was at the theater. Mark had unzipped his pants, and I had slipped my panties out from under my long dress. At some point, I said, "No. This is far enough."

Mark started crying and said, "I have to tell you something I've never told anyone before."

I was immediately receptive and open to his emotional tears. Who or what had hurt my boyfriend? "What is it? Tell me. It's okay."

"You know I had a girlfriend before I met you."

"Yes."

"We tried to have sex a few times, but I couldn't do it. We would be messing around, but I was never able to insert my penis. I think something's wrong with me."

"I'm sure nothing is wrong with you."

"I'm scared. If I just knew that I could do it, I would be okay with waiting."

My entire life, I had been taught to wait, but my concern over a possible threat to my boyfriend's manhood changed everything. I didn't wait.

Your Story

I taught high school English in the inner city of San Diego for nearly twenty years. The high school I taught at was about seventy percent

Hispanic, fourteen percent Asian, twelve percent African American, and four percent White. In the last sixteen years, I have assigned and read thousands of journal entries from these diverse students, reflecting the challenges of their individual stories. I gave students the option to fold pages in half if they didn't want me to read an entry. They knew before they ever turned in their first assignment that if I felt they were being hurt or abused in any way, or might hurt someone else or themselves, I must as a mandated reporter turn their story over to Child Protective Services (CPS). It still amazes me how many pages were not folded over, were just waiting to be read. It still amazes me the heartache and anxiety that can pour out of a teenager's fingertips.

One young girl wrote about the fear she experienced when her mother went off to work at the twenty-four-hour Mexican restaurant on 22nd and University Avenue, from six p.m. to two a.m. She was left with her father for the evening. He drank his first Taurino Cerveza when he walked in the door after working all day shoveling someone else's dirt or loading up someone else's discarded couches, chairs, or broken appliances. He frequented Del Cerro, Hillcrest, and North Park in his dilapidated truck because those neighborhoods had the money. Their rejects kept him comfortable while he made his way through a twelve-pack before the evening was over. The light would creep into this young girl's bedroom when the door was pushed ajar. She would pray and feign sleep. But it didn't matter what she said to God or what she did to try and fool her drunken father; he would overpower her delicate body time and time again.

I asked her to stay after class the next day, and shared with her my obligation to the County of San Diego. More importantly, I shared with her my concern for her safety and well-being. I shared how much I cared for her and told her that no daughter should have to protect her body from her own father. She furiously screamed,

"You have no business ruining my life! You have no idea what will happen to me!" She cried and pleaded with me not to tell.

Teachers never know what happens after we file CPS reports, and a student will rarely give up the details to an informant. The student didn't speak to me in class again, and didn't make it through the school year. A year later, she showed up in my classroom after school one day. The second I made eye contact with her, she began to cry. She walked across the room into my arms, and by the time she reached me, I was crying too. She said, "You saved my life. I just wanted you to know."

A journal entry written in pink ink with hearts on top of every "i" was written by a fourteen-year-old student who was a mother and didn't really understand how she had become one. A San Diego County health teacher had come in to teach a mandatory course on male and female anatomy, stages of dating and intimacy, sexually transmitted diseases, and contraceptives. This naïve mother wrote about how embarrassing it was to see all the pictures, and drew a pink penis next to a girl and a cartoon speech bubble, saying "penis, penis, penis." She finished the drawing with her rendition of a giggling emoji. She wrote about a party she went to in someone's garage on Chamoune Street just six blocks from school. No parents around. An advanced-level game of spin the twenty-ounce beer bottle left her as the winner. She was taken into a dark corner behind the dilapidated couch, barely slipping down her pants for the insertion of something that she had never seen before, during, or after the birth of her child.

Some of these stories might seem far from what is normal for you. Everybody has different experiences, and that's normal too. I suspect that girls in high schools across America would share just as many "sex" stories as my girls have told me. Some situations are abusive, and a young teen may feel powerless. We'll talk more about abuse and what you can do to seek help in **Chapter 16**. Some situations are more about peer pressure or the desire to be accepted and loved. The common thread across all socioeconomic, cultural or religious groups is that all girls should have access to knowledge that helps keep them safe.

Do Pregnancy Rates Go Down When Girls Have More Knowledge?

The easy answer is yes, they do. That makes me happy because when I started this project I didn't know this to be true. And to be honest, movies, television, and social media do not project this truth. It's almost like someone out there wants to convince girls that all girls love provocative clothes, enjoy giving guys whatever they want, relish in casual hook-ups that mean nothing, and adore sex . . . lots of meaningless sex. (When you think of the Me Too Movement, and how many powerful movie/TV producers are allegedly involved in coercing and abusing women, it does make you wonder, huh?)

After reading multiple studies, I found that pregnancy rates were super high when I was a teen in the '70s. They increased in the '80s and peaked in the '90s. Since the mid '90s, pregnancy rates have declined consistently every year in all states among all racial groups. All the studies agree that teen pregnancy rates are the lowest they have been in twenty years, and most agree that teens are having less sex and have become more effective contraceptive users. (We'll talk more about birth control in **Chapter 14**.)

There is still plenty of room for debate as to *why* teen pregnancy rates are so low and still continuing to drop. I'm going to give you some of the theories because I want you to be informed. But to be honest, no matter the reasons, I'm pretty sure teen girls (and boys) get a lot of the credit. Yay girls!

Education programs have taught teens to delay first sex, to reduce the frequency of sex and the number of partners, to increase contraceptive use, and to reduce sexual risk taking. But most studies agree this can't be the only factor because only a few hours of instruction a year doesn't have enough impact.

AIDS education and the effect of role models like Magic Johnson contracting AIDS and then speaking out about prevention increased the use of condoms and safety during sex. In 1995, thirty-eight percent of teens used condoms, but by 2010 seventy-five percent of teens used condoms.

Child-bearing norms changed. Women began having children later in order to finish their college education and enter the work force. Teen girls perhaps copied this trend, seeing the importance of delaying pregnancy.

Media access for teens has increased. By 2013, ninety-three percent of teens had internet access and seventy-eight percent had cell phones. Websites allow teens to ask questions they may have been too embarrassed to ask before.

U.S. medical recommendations/guidelines changed for teen examinations. Though individual clinics and providers may vary slightly, girls can now receive hormonal contraceptives and IUDs without pelvic exams or Pap tests. These two forms of contraception are more effective for teen girls than relying on oral contraceptives or male condoms. The age to be able to take the morning after pill was also lowered to seventeen. The current recommendation is that women have their first Pap and pelvic exam at twenty-one years of age.

Parent involvement makes a difference. Some studies say parents are talking to their kids more about sex now than ever before.

Media reality shows like *16 and Pregnant* and *Teen Mom* are given credit by one study, saying that seeing the reality of raising a baby when you're a teen has made a difference. Teens see how difficult it is to be a young mother and how much they have to give up.

Did You Know / Not So Fun Facts

Sexually Transmitted Diseases (STDs)

Chlamydia

Explanation:
Common STD caused by bacterial infection. Spread thru vaginal and oral sex. Carried by semen (cum), pre-cum and vaginal fluids.

Symptoms:
Usually none; get tested

Treatment:
Antibiotics

Prevention:
Use condoms or dental dams*

Genital Warts

Explanation:
Common STD caused by certain types of HPV. Carried by skin-to-skin contact with someone who's infected, often during vaginal, anal, oral sex.

Symptoms:
Skin-colored or whitish bumps on vulva, vagina, cervix, penis, scrotum or anus.

Treatment:
May go away on their own; talk to a doctor about treatment options.

Prevention:
Get HPV vaccine and use condoms to lower your chances.

Gonorrhea

Explanation:
Common STD caused by bacterial infection spread thru vaginal, anal, and oral sex. Carried in semen (cum), pre-cum, and vaginal fluids. Can affect penis, vagina, cervix, anus, urethra.

Symptoms:
Often none; get tested.

Treatment:
Antibiotics

Prevention:
Use condoms or dental dams*

	Explanation:	Symptoms:	Treatment:	Prevention:
Hepatitis B	A virus that can cause liver disease, spread thru sex or sharing personal hygiene items like razors or toothbrushes. Carried in semen, vaginal fluids, blood and urine.	Usually none; may feel like flu	No cure, but often goes away on its own.	Get Hep B vaccine and use condoms
Herpes	A common STD that infects your mouth and/or genitals. Easily spread from skin-to-skin contact with someone who has the virus. You can get it when your genitals and/or mouth touch their genitals and/or mouth, usually during oral, anal and vaginal sex.	Blistery sores.	No cure, but symptoms are treatable.	Use condoms. Do not have contact with another person's mouth or genitals if they have herpes sores.
HIV and AIDS	Infection that breaks down your immune system and can lead to AIDS. Damages immune system, making it easier for you to get sick. HIV is carried in semen, vaginal fluids, anal mucus, blood and breast milk. Spread thru vaginal or anal sex, sharing needles or fluids in open sores on your body.	Often none for many years; get tested.	No cure, but treatment can help you stay healthy.	Wear condoms; don't share needles. Ask doctor about PrEP—a daily pill that helps prevent HIV.

		Explanation:	Symptoms:	Treatment:	Prevention:
HPV (Human Papillomavirus)		Common STD with over 200 types. Sexual varieties are spread from sexual skin-to-skin contact when vulva, vagina, cervix, penis, or anus touches someone else's genitals or mouth and throat, usually during sex.	Usually none. Sometimes causes genital warts or cancer.	No cure, but vaccines help protect you. Genital warts can be removed by doctor.	Condoms and dental dams offer partial protection*
Pubic Lice (aka "crabs")		Small parasites that attach to the skin and hair near your genitals, usually spread during sexual contact.	Intense itching.	Over-the-counter medicine.	Don't have intimate contact.
Scabies		Tiny parasites that cause itching. Passed through skin-to-skin contact, usually during sex.	Rashes, irritation, itchy skin.	Medicated creams or pills.	Don't have intimate contact.
Syphilis		Common bacterial infection. Spread through vaginal, oral, or anal sex when in contact with chancres.	Sores on the genitals called chancres. Often not detected; get tested.	Antibiotics.	Use condoms and dental dams*

		Explanation:	Symptoms:	Treatment:	Prevention:
Trichomoniasis	(Trich)	Common STD causing vaginitis. A parasite that spreads easily during sex. Carried in sexual fluids like semen, pre-cum, and vaginal fluids.	Irritated vulva or vagina. Itching, smelly discharge, painful or frequent peeing.	Antibiotics for both sexual partners.	Use condoms.

*Dental dams are usually small, square sheets of latex put over the penis or vagina when having oral sex for protection against sexually transmitted infections.

Wow, that was a lot of information. Thanks for staying with me!

I wish I had access to this information back in the day . . . before I entered into a serious relationship and had sex at sixteen. No one asked me what kind of relationship and sexual experiences I wanted or didn't want for myself. No one asked me whether the choices I was making were right for me. No one asked me whether what I was doing even felt right to me. Maybe more importantly, I didn't ask myself. Listen to your hearts, girls. Even if you are not close to being in a relationship or having sex, answer some of these questions for yourself now.

What I Wish My Mama Would Have Told Me

I wish my mama would have told me about like and love and wanting to have sex. I wish she would have told me every possible way a girl could be talked into sex. I wish she would have told me that self-esteem, and the need to love someone into wholeness, and the desire to be wanted and needed by someone gets all tangled up with the desire to actually engage in the sexual act.

She didn't have to talk me out of being in love. I wish she would have talked to me about *whether* I was in love, all the reasons I loved my boyfriend and all the reasons I didn't love my boyfriend. I wish I could have told her everything that was driving me crazy about him, both positive and negative. Maybe she and I would have noticed together that my intuition was already questioning whether this guy was the right guy for my beautiful love and my beautiful self. I wish my mama would have said, "If you aren't ready to talk to me about your relationship with Mark, talk to another adult you trust who is a good listener with pretty solid judgment. Choose someone who is a good judge of character."

Maybe as my mom and I talked out why I loved and didn't love my boyfriend, *I* would have come to the realization that there were some red flags waving across my sub-consciousness. In fact, some of the red flags may have been poking me right in the eye.

Opportunities to Journal

* If you could ask one question about sex (good, bad, or ugly), what would it be?

* Are you making the decisions about sex that are right for you today? If not, what steps can you take to start over?

* After reading these stories, what concerns/questions/comments do you have?

* Jot down some notes about what you are willing and not willing to do sexually from this moment forward.

Take-Aways

* Having sex in a committed, mature relationship with a partner who truly cares for you is good.

* Objectifying girls, manipulating them, forcing them to act without full consent is bad. Having unprotected sex, making you vulnerable to pregnancy and STDs, is bad.

* Pregnancy rates go down when girls have more knowledge.

* Movies, television, and social media do not reflect the reality of how many teens are having sex. Teens are smarter than that.

* You get to decide what kind of relationship and sexual experiences you want or don't want for yourself.

* Listen to your hearts, girls. Even if you're not close to being in a relationship or having sex, know ahead of time what you will and will not do.

Chapter 14

Birth Control

Is having sex the furthest thing from your mind? Would you be embarrassed to even talk to your mom about birth control? Have you had sex once without birth control? Are you having sex regularly and want to know more about birth control? For some of you, these are heavy questions. For some of you, perhaps they're timely. All of these questions described my progression when I was a teen. One moment, sex was the furthest thing from my mind, and I would have been embarrassed to talk to my mother about it. The next minute, I had had unprotected sex and needed to know how to protect my body from pregnancy the next times I would have sex with my boyfriend.

We learned in the last chapter all the reasons why we want to be safe and protected when we do decide to have sex for the first time. We learned that sexual feelings are normal, and that sex in a committed relationship is good when we are ready. We learned some ways that girls like you and me are tricked or manipulated or taken advantage of during our first sexual encounters. We learned just how naïve and innocent we can be and how easily our childhood and virginity can be stolen away from us. We learned that more education about sex and STDs and birth control really can make pregnancy rates go down. So let's get a little more educated about birth control.

My Story

Even worse than the fact that I gave up my virginity when I didn't really want to was the fact that on that night we were both completely unprepared for sex. I thought it was so important to save him at this critical juncture that not only did we have sex in the backseat of his car in some dark parking lot, but we had sex without any birth control. Nada. Zip. Zero. Nil. Nix. Zilch. This is the moment I could have conceived a real, live baby. Sixteen years old. Two years to finish high school. I had sex with a guy who I was pretty certain—if I had been listening to at least a gazillion warnings—was not going to be the best father for the little egg under seige by a swarm of overzealous sperm.

This unwise choice happened even though there were many, many choices for birth control (and today you have even more choices). In the yearly sex-ed classes for my tenth graders, they were given over a dozen choices right out of the gate: abstinence (that means don't do it), implant, patch, pills, shot (Depo-Provera), sponge, vaginal ring (NuvaRing), cervical cap, condom, diaphragm, female condom, IUD, spermicide. And one that didn't exist for me once I finished saving my boyfriend's manhood and realized that in a few hours I could be pregnant: the morning-after pill. Girls know a lot about these different methods of birth control from the sex-ed classes they wish they didn't have to take. If not, there are many books available. There are school nurses and counselors that may be able to help. There are parents and doctors to talk to. There are many organizations available that can assist teen girls with information and planning with or without parental consent (see **Resources**). Not because she is planning to have sex today; because she is *not* planning to have sex today.

Did You Know

Birth Control & Its Effectiveness

Birth Control	What is it?	Effectiveness
Abstinence	Don't have sex	100%
Implant	A tiny rod implanted into your arm that releases hormones into the body; lasts 4 years	99%
IUD	A tiny device put into your uterus; lasts 3-12 years	99%
Shot	Depo-Provera injection; lasts 3 months	94%
Vaginal Ring	A small, flexible ring inside your vagina that releases hormones; lasts 1 month	91%
Patch	A patch worn on the skin of your belly, upper arm, butt, or back that releases hormones; lasts 3 weeks	91%
Pill	Medicine with hormones; daily	91%
Diaphragm	A shallow, bendable cap that you put inside your vagina, covering the cervix during sex; insert every time you have sex.	88%
Condom	Thin, stretchy pouch that is worn on the penis; use every time to prevent pregnancy and STDs.	85%
Female condom	Alternative to regular condoms; they go inside your vagina for pregnancy/STD prevention or inside the anus for STD prevention; use every time you have sex.	79%

Birth Control	What is it?	Effectiveness
Sponge	Small, round sponge made from soft, squishy plastic. Put it deep inside the vagina before sex; covers the cervix and contains spermicide.	76–88%
Cervical cap	A little cup made from soft silicone and shaped like a sailor's hat. Put it deep inside your vagina to cover your cervix; used with spermicide every time you have sex.	71–86%
Spermicide	Chemicals that stop sperm from reaching an egg; put inside your vagina every time you have sex.	71%
Emergency Contraception	Birth control you can use to prevent pregnancy up to five days after unprotected sex. Without a prescription you can get morning-after pills like Plan B. With a prescription you can get the copper IUD or ella morning-after pill.	89–95% Effectiveness increases the sooner you take it.

Your Story

Several years ago, I was one of the teachers in a program for junior high and high school girls that taught abstinence. Period. Just say no. Easy breezy. Okay? There. Done. The problem with abstinence as the *only* solution is that it doesn't work forever. If a girl chooses not to be on birth control, one of the major reasons—one may say—is that she is not going to have sex. Her parents believe this. She believes this. I believed this. The only factor this ideology doesn't take into account is that she *might* have sex when she least expects it. Certainly when a parent least expects it. Many of the girls in my program—and generally in my classroom on any given day—had absolutely no intention of having sex when they did for the first time. It's not enough to say you aren't going to do it. There are so many factors that lead up to that slippery moment when it's too late to take it back.

One of the girls in my program who had made a conscious decision (like me) not to have sex before she was married got pregnant when she was sixteen. She came back to our group to tell us what went wrong, which I think was a very brave thing to do.

"My boyfriend and I were at a park playing around on the playground."

They sat there amidst the equipment they had been playing on since they were children . . . does anyone besides me see the irony here?

"We began to mess around a little bit. We were kissing and feeling each other out. We had talked about having sex, but had agreed that we would just stick to kissing and touching so that we didn't have to worry about getting pregnant. Plus, I have learned a lot in this program, and I had decided that I didn't want to have sex until I was married. We never really took off our clothes because we were outside. We kind of pulled down our pants and I don't think there was any insertion, but I'm not really sure. We were both kind of in the moment and didn't realize what was happening. I missed a couple of periods. We were both so scared."

She became a mother at sixteen. One day she was playing on the playground, and the next moment she was trying to keep appointments at the clinic and stay in school while her body grew and changed. In a few months, she was changing diapers, comforting a crying baby, and figuring out how she and the sixteen-year-old father were going to raise this baby they had created while they were playing.

What I Wish My Mama Would Have Told Me

I wish my mama would have talked to me about birth control. I wish she wouldn't have just assumed that I wasn't going to have sex.

That's what I assumed too, but I didn't understand what can happen sometimes at the peak of pleasure and passion ... or even in a calculated decision. I wish she would have told me all of the whens and wheres she'd ever heard about a young woman or man first having sex, then found some more. I wish she would have realized that birth control didn't mean I would have sex, only that I would be protected if the unplanned moment arrived.

I wish she would have told me that in addition to making a decision whether or not to have sex, I could also make a decision whether or not I wanted to engage in the risky behaviors that lead to sex—like parking on a dark street, making out, drinking or taking drugs, or any other mind-altering moments when we begin to think with our body instead of our brain. I wish we would have had conversations about whether or not I was even with the person with whom I wanted to raise a baby and perhaps spend my entire life.

Opportunities to Journal

* Do you have any questions or concerns about birth control? If so, what are they?
* What further information would you like to have about birth control?
* Do you need/want to discuss birth control with your mother or another adult? (Remember, you can go to Planned Parenthood without parental consent—See **Resources**.)
* What are your fears about having birth control or not having birth control?

Take-Aways

* Deciding not to have sex does not always equate to not having sex.
* There are many birth control options to consider should you choose birth control.

* Consider talking to a doctor or someone else you trust to see if birth control is the best option for you. See **Resources** for a list of agencies who can help you.

* Birth control is free for teens, completely confidential, and you do not need parental permission.

* Just-say-no and abstinence don't take into account that you might have sex when you least expect it.

Chapter 15

Red Flags

Remember when we talked about intuition? That feeling in your gut that something is wrong or that something might happen? Intuition happens on the inside. Red flags are more obvious, more on the outside. For example, your boyfriend smashes his car door in with his bare fist when he's angry with his awful parents. You make excuses for his behavior. "This has never happened before. It won't happen again. He is under a lot of stress right now."

Literally, a red flag means caution, right? It's used in car racing when there has been an accident on the track, and cars should slow down and prepare to restart the race. A red sign on a street corner goes one step further. Stop. A red cape can mean either superhero or super sharp horns: bull approaching. Red flags can look like jealousy, possessiveness, control, isolation, selfishness, disrespect, unreliability, and physical, emotional, or social abuse.

I didn't tell anyone that my relationship with Mark was getting more intense. Or that we were having sex. Or that I was beginning to see a different Mark, one that was controlling and had a temper that could flare up with hardly a moment's notice. I had distanced myself from all of my girlfriends, and I certainly wasn't talking to my parents. I didn't know that my love could *never* change my boyfriend's actions. I didn't know that my body was trying to warn me. I didn't know that I had the power to save myself.

My Story

I think our bodies first give us warnings with nudges in the pits of our stomachs or aches in our hearts or pressure just behind our squinting eyeballs. I think that's what happened to me, but I didn't recognize that my intuition was, once again, trying to save me. The longer Mark and I were together, the more I worried that our relationship was in trouble. I felt apprehensive that I was no longer in love, but I didn't know what to do with the information. I didn't know that these feelings would turn into "red flags" trying to caution me: Warning. Danger ahead. Stop.

My red flags?

* **Red flag #1:** Riding my bike over to Mark's house and being sent away by his mother who never asked me my name or offered me a glass of water after my long ride. She simply berated me and shut the door in my face.
* **Red flag #2:** The family night of putting together Playboy puzzles and then critiquing the naked bodies.
* **Red flag #3:** Mark's parents' frequent drunkenness.
* **Red flag #4:** The violence in the family, marked by fistfights between the boys, holes in the walls, and screaming.

I never told my mother any of these tidbits of information, maybe because I suspected she would want me to break up with Mark. She would be worried that Mark would turn out that way too. But I knew he wouldn't. I could save him from his parents, and later from himself (Read more about trying to change others in **Chapter 18**). I thought that if I loved Mark enough, he would stay the shy, sweet boy I knew he really was. After all, he saw the faults of his parents, and he did not want to repeat them. My love would ensure that he became the perfect boyfriend and husband I had been dreaming of my whole life. I wish there would have been some way to stop me from running right past the red flags into an abusive marriage.

Did You Know / Not-So-Fun Facts

Dating Red Flags

Behavior	What this behavior may be showing you
Your boy/girlfriend doesn't like you hanging out with your friends.	Jealousy
Thinks your friends aren't cool enough or that their opinions, especially about him/her, are a bad influence.	Possessiveness
Is rude to your friends or family or forbids you to hang out with them.	Control; wants to isolate you from friends/family
Discourages you from pursuing your interests because he wants you to like what he likes.	Control; you may not be compatible
Demands you stop social media or wearing certain clothes, makeup, or jewelry.	Jealousy; control
Requires that you check in several times a day by text, calls, email to let him/her know what you're doing.	Jealousy; control; possessiveness
Tries to get you to stop or not even start extracurricular activities that would benefit you.	Selfishness; doesn't want what's best for you
Pressures you to do anything you are not comfortable with, physically or emotionally.	Disrespect
Doesn't keep promises, changes plans, or leaves you stranded.	Unreliability
Loses his/her temper with you (putting you down, yelling, screaming, pushing, hitting).	Abuse (see **Chapter 16**)

Your Story

When I taught seniors—seventeen, eighteen, and nineteen-year-old young adults preparing to go out into the world on their own—I heard more stories about red flags than with my younger students. Maybe students were more willing to talk and less willing to put up with domineering boyfriends and girlfriends. The girls, especially, were learning to have a voice and stand up for themselves. We had studied a book with a strong female protagonist, and some of their eyes had been opened.

But what I often found was that the *words* girls spoke were strong, but the influence of their cultures, their families, and their boyfriends were often stronger than the new concepts they were learning.

One engaging, creative Mexican-American girl—let's call her Claudia—would often be met by her boyfriend after my English class, which was her last class of the day. If he was having a good day, she would quickly gather her belongings and wouldn't stay even a few minutes to talk to classmates or to ask a question about an assignment. On the days he didn't come, it was often because they had had a fight. He was very possessive and would get mad at her for not being ready, for talking to friends, for needing to talk to me.

She was trying out the concept of standing up for herself, and realizing that she should not tolerate his controlling behaviors. She was reading the red flags.

"Mrs. J, he's too possessive. He's always mad at me and wants to control everything I do. He wants sex with me at night, but the next day at school he flirts with other girls and acts like he doesn't even know me. I know he's not good for me."

I'd share my story and say, "Follow your intuition. There will be someone else in your future who is healthier and appreciates you more. It's not too late to opt out of part or all of this relationship." We'd talk about red flags and how to watch for them and learn from them.

Within a couple of weeks, she'd be back together with him. She'd say, "I know I said I wasn't getting back together with him, but he's been so nice. I think he's really changed this time."

She came to visit me after graduation. She was pregnant ... by the same guy, who wouldn't marry her and didn't support her.

What I Wish My Mama Would Have Told Me

I wish my mama would have told me that those early red flags were not only about Mark's parents; they were also about him. Even though Mark was not his parents, he learned unhealthy behaviors from them. We've talked a little bit about this already, but it would have done me good to hear it more than once. I wish my mother would have told me, "You spend your most vulerable years with your parents. It is likely you will be pretty much the same as your parents. There is no guarantee one way or the other, true. You may have the strength and fortitude to fight a horrific childhood. People do it. But here's the most important part: Love will not change the way someone was raised."

I wonder if there would have been some way my mother could have communicated to me that my relationship with Mark was doomed for failure. I may not have listened, but let's hold on to the slim chance that I maybe, just maybe—if good communication between us had already been established—could have avoided a lot of pain and heartache. I wish my mother would have told me, first, what red flags were, and second, how to pay attention to those red flags and the lessons they were trying to teach me. Maybe I would have had the strength to take action.

Opportunities to Journal

❋ Have you ever been in a situation where you saw someone behave in a way that was unusual for him/her and you felt scared? Explain what happened.

* What message were you getting? How did that make you feel?
* What can you do about it when you begin to feel the stab of a red flag?
* Who can you talk to if you need help getting out of a situation where your intuition tells you that you are unsafe and external red flags are waving?
* When you want to opt out of a party, a date, or even a budding relationship, what are some excuses you can use? Make a list! (I always told my sons they could blame anything they wanted to on me. "My mom won't allow me to go.")

Take-Aways

* Your intuition and your physical body will give you signs *on the inside* that something is wrong with a relationship (remember **Chapter 9**)?
* Red flags are behaviors we see *on the outside* of someone else like jealousy, possessiveness, control, isolation, selfishness, disrespect, unreliability, and physical, emotional, mental and social abuse.
* Love will not change the way someone was raised or the way someone acts (see more in **Chapter 18**).
* You can choose to opt out from a date, a party, or a relationship. Your own health and well-being are the most important things.
* Pay attention to the red flags you encounter. You have the strength to take action to protect yourself.

Chapter 16

Abusive Relationships

The thing about red flags is that when they go unnoticed or unchecked, they can turn into full-on abuse. Maybe you've only seen abuse on television or in a movie. More likely you've seen signs of abuse in your daily life but may not have fully comprehended what you were seeing. Have you ever noticed that your friend's boyfriend puts her down in front of others or gets angry because of what she's wearing? Have you seen guys gathering around a cell phone and realized that they were looking at a nude photo of someone you know... or someone you don't know? Maybe you've been the victim of an unwanted touch or kiss. Abuse, especially in teen relationships, is not always easy to see.

It's confusing because we think we know what abuse looks like: It's when someone hits you or forces himself on you sexually. Yes, those are forms of abuse. But sometimes abuse is more verbal or emotional. Sometimes it's about how our partner interacts with us on the phone or on social media. We often start out in a honeymoon phase with the one we love. Then tension begins to build until we experience the first explosion of temper. After outbursts like this, Mark always said he was sorry and told me how much he loved me.

We can choose *not* to ignore these red flags. We can get ourselves out of a relationship even when we find ourselves smack dab in the middle of a hot mess. If we get caught up in a repeating cycle of calm, tension, explosion, we can put up our own red flag, talk it over with someone we trust, and leave the unhealthy relationship in the dust.

My Story

Mark and I wanted to be together every moment we possibly could. When I was a junior and Mark was a senior, he claimed me with the make-out sessions in the morning witnessed by students in the parking lot, by the hickies on my neck, and by kissing me hello and good-bye between classes with the fervor of a young lover who was going off to war. During lunch break—which used to be spent with my two best girlfriends, eating our bag lunches in the quad—we usually went to Mark's photography class to hang out with his friends. I don't remember eating food for lunch any longer.

He traded in his blue Chevy for a green Datsun with a black racing stripe. It was used, but sleek and shiny. He got a part-time job at Farrell's Ice Cream Parlour. I settled into life as the girlfriend of the cute senior guy with the new car and the job, and my life was dedicated to him. I didn't see my girlfriends at all anymore. Every extracurricular activity I was involved in now included Mark. I had no time on my own except when Mark was at work, and I usually spent those evenings doing homework or hanging out with my family. Mark wasn't the jealous type, but I suppose he had no reason to be. I was with him 100% of his available time.

When our sexual encounters became more frequent, so did our fights. I have allowed the fights to be stored in some dark place in my memory like a coffin with its lid nailed shut. When I close my eyes real tight, I feel sexual tension slipping through cracks in the wooden box.

I was frequently anxious, thinking to myself: *Where will we have sex? Will we get caught? Will I get pregnant even though we're using condoms?* Mark became bolder. I fought my own desires and his desires at the same time. I was always fearful about possible consequences.

One dark night, after a date, we were parked on one of our favorite dark streets, lips locked and hands busy. I felt pressured; Mark angrily defended himself.

"Come on, Nancy. We love each other. Let's do it."

"Not here. I'm afraid someone will catch us. I don't want to take the chance of getting pregnant."

Mark was yelling now: "Stop worrying about everything all the time! You're making me crazy! You can't get me all worked up and then not follow through!"

The more intense he got, the more I cried. The pressure was too much for me. Then one day I found the courage to say, "I think we should break up for a while. I can't take this intensity."

He drove me home, speeding around every corner, and dropped me in front of my house without walking me to the door or kissing me good-bye.

Mark showed up at my parents' church the next morning, sat in the pew next to me, and grabbed my hand. He whispered fervently that he wanted to leave the service to continue the discussion. I knew my father would be angry if I left in the middle of the church service. There was Mark's angry face, his insistent grip on my hand, my mother sitting next to us, and my father's tense face in the choir loft, where he and the other choir members faced the congregation. I could tell from my father's face that he was sensing something was not right between us, and he didn't like it one little bit.

Mark won. We left the service, got in his car, and drove to a nearby park. We argued and he began to shout.

"God dammit, Nancy! You're always so worried about what your parents think and what everyone else thinks. I'm in college now! I have needs! Everyone else in college is having sex, and I'm with a high school girl who doesn't want anything to do with me."

"Well, I'm sorry I'm just a little high school girl. Go have sex with someone else!"

"I know you don't want that. I know you want to have sex with me. Stop worrying all the time and let's have a more grown-up relationship!"

"I'm tired of your pressure! I can't have sex with you in all these weird places whenever you feel like it!"

I got out of the car at one point and leaned against the passenger door. Mark stomped around to my side of the car and proceeded to smash in the side door with his fists until it was completely dented. I was scared and, if I wasn't already crying, started to cry. I told him I needed a break from him and told him to go date some college girls.

When we returned, the church service was long over, and my father was furious. I don't remember if that was our first break-up, but after Mark's temper tantrum, I did officially break up with him. I listened to my gut, to my intuition telling me to get away.

Soon after, my sister took me out to dinner to help me feel better, and Mark was in the same restaurant with another girl. It devastated me to see him with another girl, and I called him afterwards. I told him I would get back together with him. I couldn't stand to think of him with someone else. I ignored my intuition this time and was led by my overwhelming jealousy. A dozen roses were delivered to me the next day, and the honeymoon phase began again.

Of course, I didn't know that in the discussion of abuse, Mark was the "abuser," and I was the "target." I didn't know about the honeymoon phase or other phases of abuse. A lot of research has been done on the cycle of abuse since the '70s. Some studies identify three main phases, some four, and some as many as six phases in the cycle of abuse. I taught my students three: tension-building, explosion, and honeymoon period.

Did You Know

A Three-Phase Abuse Cycle

Phase 1:
Tension-Building

During this phase there is arguing, yelling and false accusations, with the feeling that things could blow up at any moment.

Phase 2:
Explosion

The tension is released in a burst of physical, sexual and/or verbal/emotional abuse. The explosion could be screaming and yelling in a way that is scary or embarrassing; hitting, grabbing, shoving, kicking, slamming; throwing objects; threatening to hurt the target or someone he or she cares about; raping the target or forcing her to go further sexually than she wants to.

Phase 3:
Honeymoon Period

The abuser tries to make the target stay in the relationship by apologizing and promising that the abuse will never happen again; buys the target flowers or gifts; accuses the target of doing something to cause the abuse; blames the abuse on other things such as alcohol, drugs, or stress.

After the honeymoon phase, the tension starts to build again, leading to another explosion. Over time, the honeymoon phase may get shorter or even disappear and the explosions may become more violent and dangerous.

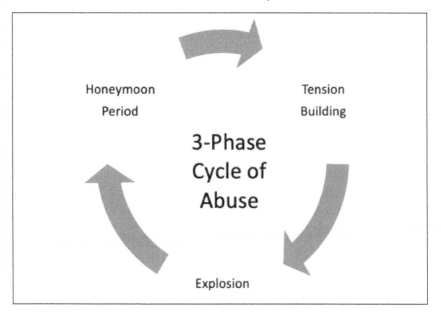

Honeymoon Period

Tension Building

3-Phase Cycle of Abuse

Explosion

Now I know that Mark was an abuser, but I don't know if I would have believed it then. After all, his Phase 1 (Tension Building) was arguing, and I just felt like I couldn't do anything right. His Phase 2 (Explosion) was screaming and yelling... but not all that scary, awful stuff like hitting or threatening or raping. He covered Phase 3 (Honeymoon) well: apologies, flowers, sweet kisses, saying "I love you," and "I'll never do it again." He would say, "You just scared me. I don't want to lose you." I thought maybe this was just how boys were. I thought I was probably frustrating him because we weren't having sex enough. I was putting a lot of stress on him.

Did You Know / Not-So-Fun Facts

Types of Abuse

Physical	Scratching, pinching, strangling, shoving, punching, burning, pushing, physical restraint, biting, pulling hair, using a weapon, spitting, kicking, choking, slapping.
Sexual	Unwanted kissing or touching, date rape, forcing someone to go further sexually than he or she wants to, not letting someone use birth control or protection against sexually transmitted infections, forcing someone to wear or not wear items of clothing (such as underwear).
Verbal/ Emotional	Name calling and put-downs, insulting the person or his/her family or friends, yelling and screaming, embarrassing the person in front of others, intimidating the person, preventing the person from seeing or talking to friends and family, telling the person what to do, making the person feel responsible for the violence/abuse, stalking, making the person feel guilty about wanting to leave the relationship by talking about the abuser's hard life and how alone and abandoned the abuser will feel if left and threatening to commit suicide.
Digital	Sexual abuse like videotaping or recording a sexual act or nude image of someone without their consent; sending someone unwelcomed sexual images; altering an image of a person to make it appear that they were posing in the nude or engaging in sexual activities; verbal/emotional abuse like sending unwanted messages of a sexual nature to someone; sending the person pornographic videos, images, or media; excessive or unwanted text-messaging, instant messaging, phone calls or emails to check up on someone; posting fake or altered images of someone or "photoshopping" a person's images.

Your Story

In my high school English classes, I taught two books as part of an abuse unit, both of which I would highly recommend. The books were called *Dreamland* by Sarah Dessen and *Breathing Underwater* by Alex Flinn. *Dreamland* is told from the viewpoint of the abused teenage girl, and *Breathing Underwater* is told from the perspective of the abusive boyfriend. In both we see their thoughts as they fall in love with their partners, but also as they begin to realize that the relationship is abusive. It's powerful to see the girl recognize abusive behaviors, but also powerful to be inside the abuser's head as he realizes what he is doing and struggles with why he is doing it.

The thing about abuse is that it's not always easy to see. Some of the warning signs we learned are as simple as jealousy, making fun of you in front of others, telling you what to do, having a bad temper, being possessive of your time, isolating you from your friends and family, preventing you from doing what you want to do, checking up on you. Some new warning signs since the advent of online platforms like Facebook, Instagram, Snapchat, TikTok, and cell phones are checking your cell phone to see who you've been talking to, deleting "friends" on social networks, altering your online profiles, using your passwords without permission, deleting files or photos the abuser doesn't like, and even pressuring you to send nude photos.

What I Wish My Mama Would Have Told Me

I wish my mama would have told me about the stages of abuse and that sometimes they're difficult to recognize. I wish she would have talked to me about what a healthy, respectful teen relationship looks like. I wish she would have talked to me about warning signs and how family, friends, and adults we trust can help keep us safe. Even if I wasn't recognizing abuse in my relationship with Mark, general conversations about signs that a relationship is not healthy or that teen dating abuse is a real thing could have influenced my trajectory. I would have liked to know that it wasn't my fault, and that I could decide to take care of myself first. I wish my mama would have told me, "Run, my love, run."

Opportunities to Journal

* Do you recognize any of the stages of abuse in your relationship or in a relationship you have observed?

* Have you experienced being controlled, yelled at, or put down by anyone? If the answer is yes, what can you do about it?

* Who can you talk to about this abuse? Do you have a safe person or a safe friend? (see **Resources.**)

Take-Aways

* Ignoring red flags can lead to an abusive relationship.

* Abuse, especially in teen relationships, is not always easy to see. It's confusing because we often think of abuse as physical, but abuse can also go unseen. Emotional, digital, and sexual abuse, for example, can be quiet and secretive.

* There are many forms of abuse including verbal, emotional, physical, sexual, and digital.

* You have the option to leave an abusive relationship. It takes bravery. Sometimes it takes telling someone and planning.

* There are phases in an abuse cycle. They include Phase 1: Tension Building; Phase 2: Explosion; and Phase 3: Honeymoon Period.

* Talking about healthy relationships and warning signs of trouble in your own relationship can help you stay safe.

Chapter 17

Violence: The Biggest, Most Dangerous Red Flag

Would you be able to hear your intuition now that we've talked about it? Will you recognize, or have you already recognized some of those red flags that tell you to stop an unhealthy relationship? I think you have the ability to hear and see the signs. What I want to ask you now, though, is will you be able to stop that relationship once the signs have turned into actions that are emotionally or verbally abusive, and even physically aggressive and violent?

I know I would have said, "Yes, of course!" when I was a teen talking with my girlfriends. But abuse—and later violent abuse— snuck up on me just as it does for one in ten teens today. And the consequences of abuse might surprise you. Abused teens are more likely to experience depression and anxiety, and engage in unhealthy or antisocial behaviors. We now know that these feelings and behaviors can be red flags that it's time to leave a relationship. There are charts in this chapter to help you stay away from or get out of an abusive relationship.

We have the choice not to ignore red flags or abuse of any kind. We have the power to end a relationship if the red flags are sneaky and we have already experienced the cycles of tension, explosions, and honeymoon periods. We do not have to tolerate abuse. We can tell someone and get help. We are never alone.

My Story

Soon after Mark graduated from high school and we had been dating for one year, he decided he wanted to move out of his parents' house and move in with a friend. He wanted to escape the constant conflict in his home and control his own life. When he told his mom about the plans, she threw him out, telling him he was disrespectful and ungrateful. In the past, Mark would have been intimidated by her expectations and demands, but this time, her outburst brought about the opposite effect. Mark spent a few nights at a friend's house and after one or two heated phone conversations, asked his parents if he could come by for his belongings.

Mark wanted me to go along because he thought his mom wasn't as likely to be violent if I was present. He rang the bell while holding tightly to my hand. When the door opened, we were both jerked inside. The door slammed behind us and the first sound I heard was the clack of the bolt turning in the lock. Mark's mom, Ruby, had a glass of wine in one hand, and a cigarette hanging from her prune-like mouth. She methodically locked every window and pulled every shade.

As my eyes adjusted to the musty, smoky room, I saw what must have been *all* of Mark's belongings strewn across the living room floor. The broken spokes and bent seat of his new ten-speed bike told the story of someone in a frenzied rage. Shards of glass that once protected my eight-by-ten senior photo predicted danger. Mark's dad, Jim, leaned in the doorway between the living room and kitchen, taking a drink of wine and a drag off his cigarette simultaneously.

No one spoke once the sealing-off began. Finally, Ruby stopped, took a long drag, and ordered Mark and me to sit down. Mark led me to an over-stuffed chair in the far corner of the room, and pulled me onto his lap, wrapping his arms around me like a shield. The torn shade behind us cast a triangular-shaped stream of light across the dingy room.

"So, big shot, how grown up do you feel now?" Ruby said as she held out her wine glass for her husband to fill.

"Mom, please, I just came to get my stuff."

"You think it's that easy? You just walk into my house, take everything I've ever given you, and you're out of here?"

"I'm just moving into an apartment, Mom. I'm eighteen. I'm not leaving you."

"Get her off your lap, and stand up like a man! Isn't that what you think you are? You stinkin' coward! Isn't that what he is, Dad, a stinkin' coward?"

At the mention of his title, Jim came to attention and swaggered over to join the debate. "A goddamn coward, he is."

With this, a grin formed across Ruby's thin lips. "If Mark thinks he's a man now, he should fight like a man. I say you and Mark fight."

She seductively glanced at her husband, coming onto him with a shake of her large breasts.

"If you win, Mark stays. If Mark wins, he leaves."

Jim strutted around the room. Ruby gave him an encouraging pat as he passed. She smiled her most licentious smile, as if this subtle foreplay would summon his veracity and strength.

I prayed, "Please, God. Let something happen to stop this."

Out loud, Mark begged his parents, "Please! Stop! This is crazy!"

Jim took one last swig of his wine, held his glass high in a toast to Ruby, winked at her, and made his way across the pile of Mark's belongings.

"Get up, and fight like a man."

Mark made one last plea. "We'll just leave for now. We'll come back and talk later. I promise. I won't move out. I'll stay here. We'll put everything back."

"Get up, you goddamn coward," Jim ordered.

Mark unlatched his hands from my waist. He protectively

pushed me into the corner of the chair.

"Since I'm already a man, you take the first punch," his dad threatened. "Hit me! Hit me, you goddamn pussy!"

Mark and his dad were about the same size, but it would never be an equal contest to fight against a parent, especially one that was drunk. Tears rolled down Mark's face. His fists clenched at his sides. His father leaned into his face. Mark's shaking fist cocked back, and struck his dad in the jaw.

Mark's dad never fully regained his footing as he stumbled behind his son's blow, across the piles in the living room. He landed near the front door. Blood gushed where shards of glass from my photo had sliced Jim's forearm open.

Mark's brothers dashed out of hiding in answer to their mother's screech of instructions. They all left in a flurry to go to the hospital. We later found out Jim received seventeen stitches in his arm. Ruby said nothing to Mark on her way out the door.

Mark and I cowered in the dark corner. We held each other tightly. Neither of us dared move or even cry. The beacon of light that previously entered through the torn shade had faded away as well. The room was completely dark.

When we were certain the headlights from the family station wagon had backed out of the driveway, we loaded Mark's broken and bloody belongings into his car.

It wouldn't be that many years into the future that Mark, in a fit of anger, broke a lamp in our house with his bare fist, requiring stitches just like his father had. It was the last time he ever set foot in our home.

Did You Know/Not-So-Fun Facts

When Abuse Turns Violent

Physical Violence	Hurting or trying to hurt a partner by pushing, shoving, grabbing, hitting, kicking, or using another type of physical force.
Sexual Violence	Forcing or attempting to force a partner to take part in a sex act or sexual event (like sexting) when the partner does not or can not consent.
Psychological Aggression	The use of verbal and nonverbal communication with the intent to harm another person mentally or emotionally and/or exert control over another person.
Stalking	A pattern of repeated, unwanted attention and contact by a partner that causes fear or concern for one's own safety or the safety of someone close to the victim.
Digital Abuse	Repeated texting or posting sexual pictures of a partner online without consent.

Your Story

When an abusive teen relationship becomes violent, there are often signs of the phases of the abuse cycle. We may see abuse in any one of the areas we talked about in **Chapter 16**: physical, sexual, verbal, emotional, digital. One or both partners may have been exposed to violence in their own homes like Mark was.

When we are young and just starting to begin our teen relationships, we may think teasing, name-calling, sarcasm in texts and put-downs on social media are funny, normal ways to communicate. But the truth is, if you see the early signs of abuse, you will likely experience more abuse as the relationship progresses. The patterns can become more and more abusive and violent as the relationship becomes more intimate. Surveys, like the ones I gave my high school students every year (performed by Centers for Disease Control and Prevention and other agencies), are taken anonymously and show that I am not the only teen that stayed with a boyfriend who did not turn out to be Prince Charming. In fact, about one in ten teens report some form of physical dating violence, sexual dating violence, stalking, or digital violence. Often teens do not know how or when to tell someone that their relationships have gotten out of control. These teens are more likely to experience depression and anxiety; engage in unhealthy behaviors like smoking, drugs, alcohol and eating disorders; exhibit antisocial behaviors like lying, theft, bullying or hitting; or think about suicide.

Did You Know

How to Stay Away from Abusive Relationships

Watch for red flags	End a relationship early if there are too many red flags, or if your relationship begins to cause you depression or anxiety.
Stop the cycle	If you are cycling through tension, explosions and honeymoon periods, stop the cycle when the tension begins to build again. Don't wait for the honeymoon period.
Foster healthy relationships	Connect with family, friends and role models such as teachers, coaches, mentors and youth group leaders. Don't give those relationships up for anyone.
Tell someone	Tell a trusted adult. Don't let your embarrassment or anxiety stop you from being safe.
Make a pact	Decide with another teen that you will go together for help should this happen to either of you.
Don't tolerate abuse of any kind!!	You won't move on to a violent relationship if you don't tolerate any form of teasing, put-downs, name-calling, or inappropriate social media!
Resources	Contact help lines such as National Resource Center on Domestic Violence (NRCDV), National Teen Dating Abuse Helpline at 1-800-799-SAFE (7233) (see **Resources**).

How to Get Out of an Abusive Relationship

So, let's say you're way beyond "How to Stay Away from Abusive Relationships" and smack dab in the middle of one. First and foremost, you have the right to be in a healthy, safe, supportive relationship. Abuse, in any form, is never okay. Violence from another person is never your fault. If you are having concerns because you have gone from noticing a few red flags to being physically, mentally, or sexually abused by a partner or anyone else, there are some steps you can take to make a safety plan.

How to Get Out of an Abusive Relationship

Create a Safety Plan

These ideas are put in the form of questions because you are the only one who is in control of your situation. Look for just one step you can take today to get out of your abusive relationship and find a better, safer, more loving life.

S   What is the **safest** way to get to and from school?

A   What friend(s) can I **ask** to walk with me to and from school, between classes, and to after-school activities?

F   What **family, faculty and friends** do I trust and can consider telling about the violence and abuse?

E   What is my **emergency exit** plan from school or home (if my abuser is at home)?

T   Can I **tell** someone I trust where I'm going or what I'm doing so that I can keep myself safe?

Y   **You** are the most important person in your life. Ask yourself these questions: Can I see that I deserve a healthy, safe, supportive relationship? Can I see that the abuse is not my fault?

P   Where are **places** that are safe and unknown to my abuser? If stranded, who could get me there?

L   Can I break up with my abuser? Can I make a plan to **leave**, one step at a time?

A   Can I **avoid** contact of any kind with my abuser and get a restraining order if necessary?

N   Can I change **numbers** and accounts my abuser knows and keep a list of numbers I can call when depressed or scared?

These ideas may seem overwhelming. Here's the Quick and Dirty version:

- Call National Teen Dating Abuse Helpline (1-800-799-SAFE (7233).

- Tell an adult or friend you trust.

- Pick a secret location to go to for safety when necessary.

- Trust your intuition and create a plan.

- You deserve a safe, healthy relationship.

Breaking up with a boyfriend or girlfriend or getting away from an unsafe relationship (even at home) is always difficult, but breaking up with someone who is abusive can be scary and maybe even dangerous.

In some circumstances, you may choose to break up in a public place and have a friend with you. In some circumstances, it's not safe to let your partner or your abuser know you are going to break up or leave. You may choose to go to a safe location and think about options for how to continue on with your life. If you are unsure whether to tell your boy/girlfriend that you are breaking up, you can call the National Teen Dating Abuse Helpline and they will help you decide the safest choice for you.

Even though you have seen red flags and experienced abuse or violence, you may still love your abuser. You may be worried about threats that have been made against you or others you love should you break up. You will likely miss those honeymoon periods we've already talked about. You may feel lonely and sad, but hold on to the decision you made and spend more time with family and friends who love and support you. You deserve a whole and happy life.

What I Wish My Mama Would Have Told Me

I wish my mama would have told me that when children have been encouraged to solve problems with violence from a young age, it's probably going to be very difficult for them to find peaceful resolutions to problems when they're older. When children learn to judge harshly, to challenge authority, and to use brawn over brain, it is going to be difficult for them to assimilate into society as adults. I wish my mama would have told me that Mark's past would be very difficult for him to overcome. Instead, a year later, when Mark's parents still refused to acknowledge him as their son, my father went to that same dark living room to plead with them to attend our wedding. I was eighteen, and Mark was nineteen. We had already survived many abuse cycles and were looking forward to the next honeymoon.

Opportunities to Journal

* Describe a time when you questioned how parents were teaching their child or treating their child. What were you feeling?
* From watching your friends/partners and their parents, have you realized anything about yourself and your own beliefs and values?
* Describe a time when you witnessed a violent act or a situation that could have turned violent.
* Jot down some ideas for a safety plan should you need one. What adult would you tell? What friend could you make a pact

with to help each other should this happen to either of you? Where would your safe location be? Jot down some numbers of friends, family members, or helplines.

Take-Aways

* One in ten girls miss or ignore the warning signs that they are entering into an abusive/violent relationship.

* Abused teens are more likely to experience depression and anxiety, and engage in unhealthy or antisocial behaviors. If you are experiencing these feelings or behaviors, you can seek help to leave the abusive relationship.

* Don't ignore red flags or abusive behaviors of any kind. Even teasing, name-calling, sarcasm, or put-downs can lead to more abusive behaviors.

* You can make a safety plan to leave an abusive relationship. Your safety plan could include telling someone you trust, asking for help from friends, identifying emergency exits, locating safe places, and avoiding contact with the abuser.

* End a relationship if you see too many red flags or experience cycles of tension, explosions, or honeymoon periods.

* You are not alone. Do not tolerate abuse. Tell someone. You are deserving of a healthy relationship (see **Resources**).

Chapter 18

Trying to Change Someone Else

Have you ever ignored really good advice because you think you know better? Maybe your friends were telling you that a boy wasn't good enough for you, but you thought, "They just don't understand him like I do." Have you ever thought, "If I love my boyfriend enough, I can save him from his parents and even from himself?" I truly believed that what was wrong with Mark had everything to do with his parents and nothing to do with him. The anger, the dishonesty, the manipulation, the abuse; all of those traits came from his parents, not from his sweet self.

What I would learn later is that when we are in the honeymoon period of relationships, we focus on what we have in common, on everything we love about each other. We don't want to focus on the behaviors or values we don't agree with, like the flash of anger and disrespect that one time. We justify or take responsibility for making him angry. We may find ourselves saying, "It was my fault," or "He wouldn't have acted that way if his coach/boss/parents/teacher hadn't upset him." Maybe there is that one thing that worries us a little bit or makes us anxious or makes us feel a little insecure about ourselves. For me, those little feelings grew into big feelings, and the behaviors that used to belong to just his parents suddenly (or not so suddenly) belonged to him.

My Story

After the violent exit from his parent's home, Mark settled in an apartment. I graduated from high school in June. We had broken up a few times in our two-year courtship, but I knew we could make something of our lives together. When Mark asked me to marry him, I began to make plans for a December wedding. I evaluated our relationship in terms of who his parents were—and the signs that he might have similar traits—and who Mark would be once I was his wife.

I looked at my boyfriend's parents and thought,

I can save him from them.

I looked at their drinking habits and thought,

I'm so glad Mark isn't a drinker. (I forgot he was only nineteen and hadn't really had the opportunity to be a drinker yet.)

I looked at the peek I was given into their sexual entertainment and their disrespect for a woman's body and thought,

I am so grateful Mark isn't like that.

I looked at their dishonesty and manipulation and thought,

I'm so glad Mark is honest and loving.

I looked at their self-centeredness and total disrespect for other cultures, religions, and people in need and thought,

Thank you, God, Mark isn't like that.

I looked at Mark's temper and thought,

It's just a learned behavior, a reaction to life with his parents. He will have nothing to be angry about once he is with me instead of them.

I looked at his low self-esteem about school, work, and goals and thought,

I can love him enough to build his confidence. I can change every bad thing that ever happened to him with the power of my love.

It didn't work.

Mark and I were married in December. I was eighteen. He was nineteen. He continued to work at the ice cream parlour, and I went to community college. We didn't have much money, but there was the love. And a lot of sex that didn't always feel like love. And—it turns out—a lot of arguments. Whenever we disagreed about something, Mark yelled. Sometimes he yelled about bosses before and after he was fired. Sometimes he yelled about my lack of support and understanding. His yelling escalated until he was screaming. Then he punched holes in the walls.

I cried. At first I cried because my feelings were so hurt that he yelled at me. Then I cried because I couldn't believe he had treated me like that. It just wasn't right. I thought to myself, *This isn't how husbands and wives talk to each other.* Finally, I argued and yelled and screamed right back. I got pretty good at it. But issues were never resolved. The fights often went into the night and ended in a stuffy nose and stifled sobs. And sometimes Mark would leave.

At first when Mark left, he would go to a friend's house or to his frequent Mustang club meetings where there were always lots of guys, girls, and beer. Later he found comfort in one of those car club girls . . . then the girl that he worked with at the bowling alley . . . then the girl who cut his hair. We separated for a while, but he came home with red roses saying, "You've always been the only girl for me." I got pregnant in between affairs, and he finally left for good when our baby was four months old. (Note: The final fight involved screaming in the middle of the day, punching a glass lamp, and a trip to the emergency room where multiple stitches put his arm back together. Sound familiar?)

I was twenty-three years old. I had spent seven years of my life trying to change my boyfriend. Each time he didn't change his behaviors—even after the flowers and the promises—there was a little voice in the back of my head that said, *Mark is acting very much like his parents did that night many years ago in the darkness of the living room. It's likely he is never going to change.* I ignored that voice for a long time. Final evaluation?

Holes in walls? Check.
Lots of drinking? Check.
Sexual entertainment? Check.
Dishonesty and manipulation? Check.
Broken glass and stitches? Check.

Your Story

Marielle was a sixteen-year-old student I met in my English class. She would come into my classroom during my prep period (when she should have been in math class) to talk to me when things were not going well with her boyfriend. She chose my prep period because she knew I would be in my classroom alone, and her boyfriend wouldn't know she was talking to me while he was in class. She couldn't come before school, during lunch, or after school because he was at her side every second of the day. She told me how much she loved her boyfriend and how much he loved her. She was often in tears during these sessions, afraid and frustrated. Many times, he had shoved her or slapped her during their passing period because he didn't like something she had said or the way she had looked at someone else.

Her journal entries told the story of how he had scoped out the canyon behind our high school, directly across the street from those fancy Talmadge homes, and found a cozy place where the two of them could have sex, a different period every day so no one would catch on. Sometimes the school narcs (police) would check the canyon, so he would have to choose a secluded alley off Highland or the romantic spot underneath the stairwell of the 200 building. Her story didn't stop with the great sex. She went on to say that sometimes he would slap her, punch her, or give her a shiner. But he promised to stop. I didn't have to wonder if her facts were true; I could see the evidence myself.

She would come in, mascara smeared by the tears running down her face.

"Mrs. J, can I talk to you?"

"Of course. Come on in. What's going on? Are you okay?"

"It's just that David gets so mad sometimes. I try to make him happy and do whatever he wants, but he has a really bad temper."

"We've talked about this before, right? Tell me what you're thinking today."

"Most of the time everything is so great, but I think he might have a problem with anger. He just shoved me against the wall and slapped me in the face because I didn't want to miss class to go have sex. I told him I couldn't miss any more math or I was going to fail the class. Now I'm missing class anyway."

"Remember how we've talked about warning signs that a girl or boy might be in an abusive relationship."

"Yeah."

"Okay. Let's take a look at the abuse wheel." I went to my file cabinet and got a copy for her and highlighted the facts about whether a girl can save her boyfriend from himself. "Do you think it's time to get some help for yourself?"

She started crying again and nodded "yes."

I had previously filed a report with CPS. They informed me there was already a report on file, confirming that other teachers knew as well. I reminded her about the reports and encouraged her not to stay with him. I told her I would walk her to the counselor's office. She refused, but said she would think about everything we had talked about.

They were both in my English class, and the next day they walked in with their usual strong, defiant attitude. David smiled at me and loudly said, "What's up, Mrs. J?" Marielle said, "Yeah, Mrs. J. What's up?" They took their seats on opposite sides of the room where I had placed them. I had a second at one point to whisper to her, "Is everything okay?" She answered, "I don't know what you're talking about. Mind your own business."

The bottom line was she would do anything for him. I understood her answer, and saw my teenage self in her honeymoon face. Both Marielle and my teen self from so long ago were afraid to be alone. We were afraid that no one else could love us like our boyfriends. Today, her boyfriend was treating her well, and she knew that she could save him this time around the cycle.

Did You Know / Just the Facts, Please

Girls Can't Change Guys

What Girls Say When They Think They Can Change Guys

- I believe my love can save or change him.

- I see the hurt little boy underneath.

- I recognize the pain under his behaviors or addictions.

- I am attracted to his passion and the attention he gives me.

- I can see his potential and possibility.

- I am attracted to the challenge of saving his life.

Why Girls Shouldn't Try to Change Guys

- It's not possible to change someone else and it's exhausting trying.

- We only have the power to change ourselves.

- Some character flaws are hereditary and we cannot change someone else's heredity (addiction falls into this category).

- Only two options exist: 1) Accept your boyfriend exactly as he is, or 2) Admit that you don't have magical powers to change him and end it!

- You are worthy of a peaceful, loving relationship and if you're trying to change this one, it's probably not the right one.

- You deserve someone who has the same values and goals that you do.

- You are enough exactly as you are . . . even if you're alone for a while.

- It is not your job to fix anyone else; honor that your boyfriend can fix himself.

- Take the love you think it would take to change someone else and feel it for yourself!

What I Wish My Mama Would Have Told Me

I wish my mama would have told me that no matter how much I loved my boyfriend, I couldn't cure or correct his character defects . . . and he in turn couldn't cure mine. I wish she would have told me that I had no control over another person's anger or violence. I wish my mama would have told me that I can't make someone love me by loving him more. I could never be so good in bed that he would forget all the other women. I wish she would have told me to keep my eyes wide open for the signs that one terrible scene with fighting and glass and screaming could repeat itself many years later. Mark would become his parents. Had she warned me, I still may not have listened right away, but maybe I would have gotten out faster.

Opportunities to Journal

✻ Make a list of "deal-breakers." What would make you absolutely NOT stay in a relationship with someone (or even go out with him)? If you know the deal-breakers ahead of time, you can be stronger when that cute guy eyes you. (**Examples:** Aggressive, mean, drinks too much, takes drugs, different attitude about religion or politics, spends too much money or not enough money, is disrespectful or rude, doesn't like your family and/or friends, doesn't want to spend time with you.)

✻ Describe a time when you tried to change someone's way of thinking or acting. Did it work? Why did you do it?

✻ Do you think you can change your boyfriend? Why or why not?

* Why do you think girls stay in relationships that are not good for them? What is the fear deep down inside that keeps them there?

Take-Aways

* Girls cannot change guys. (Likewise, guys cannot change girls.)
* Some character flaws are passed on through DNA; looking at your partner's parents might give you some clues to who he will become.
* Being good enough in bed, sexy enough, perfect enough does not make your partner love you more. You *are* enough. He's looking for something you cannot give him.
* Girls try to change guys because they think their love will save the hurt little boy underneath his unhealthy behaviors.
* You are worthy, deserving, and capable of choosing a peaceful, exciting, loving relationship with someone who has the same goals and values that you do.

Chapter 19

Fair Fighting

Fighting in any relationship is normal. Fighting happened in my relationship with Mark. A lot. Because my parents never fought in front of me, I didn't know what fair fighting looked like. I just thought people who liked each other—and certainly people who loved each other—didn't fight. Maybe you have been in the middle of a scary fight with a friend or significant other where your stomach was in your toes and you wished there was a hidden door so you could escape. Maybe your parents don't fight at all in front of you, like my parents . . . or maybe they have heated exchanges that make the house quake . . . or maybe you have been lucky enough to witness fair fighting where both partners speak their minds, hear the other person out, and come to satisfying resolutions.

In this chapter, we will be looking at the infinite possibilities between screaming and the silent treatment. It's easy to recognize scary fighting, and it's easy to recognize uncomfortable silence. Neither scenario is healthy. It's harder to negotiate the space in between. When do we take a stand? When do we wait until the next day when emotions are calmer? Learning to fight fair means staying away from the extremes and learning about compromise, negotiation, privacy, and respect.

My Story

I was terrified early on in our marriage when Mark screamed at me. I tried to just be quiet and wait for the storm to subside, but it rarely did. I learned pretty quickly to fight using the same strategies Mark used: yelling, blaming, and defending. His strategies didn't work, though, and never resolved anything. By the end of the argument, Mark would leave. Only when he was gone did I allow myself to cry until I fell asleep on my wet, snot-soaked, mascara-blackened pillow. There was no apology the next day. We just acted like it never happened.

After seven years with Mark, you'd think I would have learned a thing or two about what not to do when communicating, but I didn't. All during high school, I had only ever had one boyfriend. His style of fighting was the only kind of fighting I knew. I had survived some gnarly fights with Mark and acquired some bad communication habits.

I was a single mom at twenty-three. I dated over the next couple of years, but was scared to be in another serious relationship. When I finally did date someone consistently, that first fight was inevitable. I didn't really think it was a fight. He did. In my fighting experience, the exchange couldn't be defined as a fight. (His name was Tom. Full disclosure: He later became my husband and lifetime partner.)

Tom was looking for something in the kitchen, and by the time he found what he was looking for, every cupboard door in the kitchen was open. I don't remember anything from my past about kitchen doors and the importance of closing them, but I made a pretty big deal about it. In fact, I went up to him and pounded my fists on his chest.

"Why can't you just close the cupboard doors when you're finished?"

He took my fisted hands in his.

"I don't like being hit."

"I'm not hitting you. I'm just playing. It's just so frustrating. You're always leaving the cupboard doors open, and I have to follow you around shutting them."

"I'm not always leaving cupboard doors open, and you don't have to shut them. I'll see that they are open, and I'll shut them myself. You don't have to follow me around."

"Are you seriously getting angry over the fact that I found a playful way to tell you to close the cupboard doors?"

"That did not feel playful to me. You were hitting me."

"Wow. I think you are totally overreacting!"

"I don't. I'm leaving now. If you think you can be in a loving relationship with me in the future, you know where to find me."

He walked right out the front door, and I watched him get into his truck. I told myself during the next week that it was too soon for me to be in a relationship anyway. I'd just take a break. Clean slate. No boys.

It took two weeks for me to realize that I missed him, and he was not going to call me or come back. After the second week, I got in my car and went to the gas station where he worked at the time.

I pulled my car over to the side of the gas station, away from the pumps, got out of my car, and leaned against the door. He finished with a customer—back in the day when there were attendants at gas stations who pumped your gas—and made his way over to me.

When he walked towards me, his smile lit up my world. I didn't have to say one word before he gave me a big hug and said, "I thought you'd never get here."

I wish I could say that was the last time I "fought" inappropriately, but it wasn't. We would get into the same knock-down, drag-out conversations with no resolution. I had a man who loved me for all the right reasons, though, and after a communications class at our local community college, some counseling, and other recovery programs, we learned how to fight fair and with less angst. There are a bazillion books on the subject of communication. I've read many. Tom and I learned some powerful techniques from classes, books, therapy, and recovery. Here's some of what we learned:

Did You Know

Learning to Fight Fair

B   **Before** you begin talking, breathe and establish some ground rules. Ask yourself, "How important is it?" or "Why am I getting so upset?"

R   **Reflect** on one issue at a time with specific points.

E   **Express** your feelings with words and "I" statements (not actions).

A   **Avoid** extremes like silent treatment or screaming and name calling. Crying is okay. Explain to the non-crier, if necessary, that tears are not manipulation. Explain that you are sad or exhausted or afraid and you just need to cry. If you are crying to manipulate, stop it. It's not nice.

T   **Take** turns talking in a normal voice. **Think** before you speak so that you can calm yourself down. Ask yourself if what you are about to say is Thoughtful, Helpful, Intelligent, Necessary and Kind.

H   **Halt** when you need to. Are you Hungry, Angry, Lonely, or Tired? Have a time out when you need to cope with your emotions. It's smart and brave to know yourself well enough to know you need a break. It's the number one thing to do when a situation gets too heated.

E   End with compromise, understanding, or a mutual solution where both partners' needs are met. Unless one of you is busy coping. Then wait. Possibly until morning. It will be better when the sun rises again.

Your Story

I interviewed Kennedy, a tall girl with long, auburn hair and a vivacious smile. She was twenty-two, having graduated from high school four years ago. We began talking about our parents and the way they fought or didn't fight. At first, she said she didn't recall seeing her parents fight. She heard them complain about their problems, and sometimes they would give each other the silent treatment. Kennedy didn't usually know what the silences were about. The more we talked, the more she remembered one particular communication pattern between her parents. The more she recognized the pattern in her parents, the more she recognized it in herself, especially in her current relationship. We'll get back to that in a minute.

When she thought more about her parents—and then herself—she recognized that her father controlled the conversations in the household. Both she and her mother were afraid of his reactions, so they learned to stuff their feelings. Kennedy learned subconsciously that the man controlled the relationship, and that the woman's job was to please the man. For example, if Kennedy's mom—we'll call her Stella—brought up an issue, Kennedy's dad—we'll call him Bill—would smile and appear as if the issue was no big deal. He would say, "You do you," dismissing her concern.

But if Stella continued to make her point or voice her concern, he would become judgmental towards her and pick her arguments apart until Stella would retreat in silence. He did not try to understand Stella's point of view. If Stella persisted instead of being silent, Bill would have one of two reactions. He would either try to make the situation funny and become the "fixer" so she would be happy again, or he would pack a bag and leave the house.

What this communication style led to in Kennedy's home is that she did not want to communicate with her father at all. On the one hand, he was playful and funny. She loved him when he was this happy guy, and would do anything she could to keep him that way. She would only talk about the positive parts of her life like her good grades, school activities, and other personal accomplishments. But if she had a concern, she felt like she was walking on eggshells.

"If I took the conversation just one tiny step too far, he would become angry and accuse me of being ungrateful and irresponsible. He would yell, 'Get out of my face! I don't want to talk to you. If I'm not being respected, I'll just leave.' He would ignore me and act like I was a problem." Kennedy learned that his feelings mattered, but hers and her mom's didn't. Again, better to stuff your feelings.

Kennedy talked about the influence of her home communication pattern on her close friendships from high school. She said, "In high school, I became a people pleaser. I agreed with whatever my friends wanted. If I did try to voice a difference of opinion and a friend disagreed with me or got mad, I would immediately back down. I didn't know how to voice my problems the 'right way.' I didn't want to talk when I was too emotional or too upset. Instead, I became a pushover. I was afraid of their reactions, so it was better to say nothing."

In the years after high school, something switched in Kennedy. She said, "I flipped the script. I shut down any emotional conversations. If it wasn't something I could fix, I didn't want to talk about it. I started being a jerk to my friends. I mirrored my parents' relationship and their communication habits."

Kennedy currently is in a serious relationship with Chris, someone with whom she'd like to spend the rest of her life. In the beginning of their relationship, when Chris would bring up a difficult topic, Kennedy would pick it apart until Chris was confused and frustrated. Chris told her that her way of communication bordered on abuse. Kennedy said, "If he showed any emotion, I didn't know how to respond." She left the relationship twice.

"The whole thing exploded in my face. The last time I left, Chris would not take me back. We texted and messaged each other, and he was able to say everything on his mind without me manipulating or threatening him. I read everything he said, and it finally made sense to me. I finally understood that I was not an emotionally healthy person."

Kennedy worked on her relationship with Chris. She told me, "I stopped acting like I was okay. I admitted that I needed help. Our friendship came back first. Our relationship improved."

Here are Kennedy's top three tips in order to fight fair: 1) Develop the power to listen. Let someone speak and finish; 2) Don't just hear what the person is saying. Strive to understand; 3) Just picture yourselves as two people existing in the moment. One person does not have to be the aggressor and one the victim.

Did You Know

Fighting in the Age of Social Media

Where/how teens fight:

- Some teens do all their communicating, fighting and breaking up on social media.

- Some know the pitfalls of social media and refuse to fight there.

- Some find it easier to argue or break up by texting or social media so they can say what they need to say without seeing the anger or heartbreak on the person's face.

Reasons that teens fight with their significant other (SO):

- I expect to hear from my SO at least once a day or more. If I don't, I get frustrated.

- I can see that my girlfriend is tweeting, but she doesn't answer my text. I feel ignored.

- My boyfriend said his mom took away his phone, but I saw him like something on Instagram. So, what's up?

- I sent a message to my SO and I know he got it because Facebook says "seen," so why wasn't he answering me?

- My boyfriend gets jealous when someone "likes my pictures" or talks to me too much. He starts arguments online. It's embarrassing.

The teens I interviewed who were still in high school shared their feelings about fights that happen when texting or on social media. They recognized that it wasn't smart to stalk your SO's comments or to argue online. Most thought that if two teens want to argue, they should at least message each other and not put it in comments. They also mentioned that one partner should never complain about the other in tweets or any other kind of social media. Disagreements should be private. Some even said that the entire relationship should be kept off of social media, including letting people know their status has changed. Posting a status change opens the relationship up to the public, and when there is a break-up and that status changes again, everyone will want to know the details.

The last point we talked about was break-ups. Most teens agreed that break-ups should be done in person, or at least by phone. They did understand breaking up by text, though, because, "It's hard to see their reaction. We don't like to deal with seeing the person's face when we break up with them."

After the break-up is more difficult now too, because a teen has to watch her ex interact with others on social media or see old pictures of herself happy with the other person. Teens talked about some angry partners posting everything bad about their SO and why they broke up. Some continue to stalk the other person and post negative comments. One teen talked about how difficult it is to have everyone asking details because they see the status has changed. There is no privacy.

FAIR FIGHTING

Especially for teens and their friends/SOs

DO	DON'T
Use "I" statements.	Swear or use put downs.
Look at your *own* part.	Get defensive.
Take a break for an hour or a day.	"Fight" when in a bad mood.
Talk face to face.	Argue by text.
Keep your relationship private.	Share your problems on social media.
Spend time sharing face to face, even if you know the relationship is ending.	Break up by text or social media.
Be productive: "When you ___, I feel ___."	Use accusatory statements: "You always ___" or "You did this or that."
Learn from each "fight." Try to remember what upsets the other person.	Push each others' buttons.
Seek help if you are feeling unsafe.	Ever put up with physical, emotional, or mental abuse.

FAIR FIGHTING

Especially for parents and their teens

DO	DON'T
Use "I" statements and express feelings.	Use "you" (You do this or that).
Notice what's working and not working.	Use absolutes like always, never, must.
Respect your teen's point of view.	Cuss or name call.
Keep your body open and relaxed.	Cross your arms, finger-point or ball up fists.
Talk in a normal voice.	Yell or scream.
Take a break if you're too angry.	Hit.
Stay in the present moment on the present issue.	Bring up the past.
Let your teen express her/himself.	Interrupt.
Listen for your teen's need. Seek to understand.	Assume you're right.
Pick your battles. Teens will pay more attention when it's important.	Focus on the "small stuff."
Let your teen "own" their problems. Ask how he/she plans to fix the problem or choose a consequence.	Stress over their grades, relationships, or problems.
Forgive and move on. Remember the goal was to resolve something.	Hold a grudge.

What I Wish My Mama Would Have Told Me

I wish my mama would have told me that fighting happens in a relationship. To have a fight doesn't mean you're a failure. It doesn't mean the relationship is over. It doesn't mean you have to scream and cry and cuss and blow your nose until your head is going to explode. I wish she would have told me that there is a healthy way to fight—somewhere between not fighting at all (like my parents) and screaming and yelling and hitting things (like Mark's parents). I wish she would have told me that sometimes it's hard to communicate. I wish she would have modeled difficult conversations. I wish my mama and I would have had rambunctious verbal spars where we each struggled to make our points . . . so I could have practiced.

There's one last thing I need to discuss about fair fighting and communication and every decision you will ever make in your life. I wish my mama would have told me that there are many shades of gray between white and black. I am pretty good at seeing the "good" choice and the "bad" choice, but I am still working on the fact that there are many choices in between. Maybe living in this world of extremes is what made it so difficult for me to learn about fair communication.

What are the choices between "I don't want to go to the movies and you do," or "I don't want to go to college and you want me to," or "I don't want to have sex and you do?" There are many shades of negotiation. We will need the skills of negotiation out in the worlds of education, work, and finance. Sometimes we will get along, and sometimes we won't. In between absolute love and complete frustration, there are many emotions and lessons and possibilities.

Opportunities to Journal

* Describe a fight you had with a parent, friend, or boyfriend. Would you describe it as fair fighting? What could you have done differently?
* Have you ever started out fighting about one thing and ended

up fighting about something totally unrelated? Explain the argument and what you could have done differently to keep the discussion on one issue.

* Are there certain topics that "push your buttons" and always make you want to fight? Write them down and explore why these topics are "hot topics" for you.

* Have you ever called someone names during an argument or been called names yourself during an argument? How did that make you feel?

Take-Aways

* Fighting is normal in a relationship.

* Learning to fight fair means staying away from the extremes (not talking at all vs. screaming and name-calling) and learning compromise, negotiation, and waiting until you both are calmer.

* Many teen fights are a result of expectations and disappointments related to cell phones and social media.

* Disagreements and break-ups should be kept private and face to face.

* Communication can be hard and requires negotiation skills that will serve you, not only with your partners, but out in the worlds of education, work, and finance.

Chapter 20

Money Matters

Do you ever wish you had more money for a new outfit or a school activity? Have you ever brainstormed about a part-time job or some other way of earning money? Maybe parents and/or grandparents have gifted you money for that special trip or opportunity that is outside most teen budgets. Maybe you have asked your parents or grandparents to loan you money for that starter car or summer band trip to NYC.

You can be reliable and diligent in paying family members back for the times they helped you. You can ask your parents if you can participate in the family budget. You can start your own system of tracking personal expenses and saving for a car or future college expenses. You can choose how you want to spend your money and what is most important to you.

It's never too soon to learn the power that comes from being financially responsible. Technology and the gig economy provide teens endless opportunities to be entrepreneurs. At the same time, technology provides easy opportunities to spend at the click of a key or an "add to cart" button. Finding a balance between spending vs. saving and cash vs. credit is important to reduce stress and live an abundant life.

My Story

When I married Mark, we recorded the incoming paychecks, subtracted rent, groceries, and gas, and thought we had plenty left over. We didn't even consider saving for the unexpected, for our future family, for our retirement. We found that we could get whatever we wanted on credit as long as the income minus the payments for living and credit cards equaled zero. But that scenario didn't take into consideration all of life's problems and responsibilities that are right around the corner: car maintenance and repairs, medical and dental bills, holiday and birthday gifts, saving for a house or a new car or children.

And then there was the dishonesty. Instead of saving for a new car, Mark and his family conspired to defraud his parents' car insurance company. We were newly married, and Mark's car was still on his parents' insurance. He parked his car in an alley downtown one night, and he and his father snuck back in the dark to set the car on fire. They reported it to the insurance company, the car was totaled, and Mark got a new car. I learned about what happened by overhearing his brothers brag about it.

A couple years later, I was in a car accident. I had to go to a chiropractor for several months. The chiropractor didn't expect me to pay at the time, knowing that the insurance company would settle after my neck had healed. To my knowledge, the insurance check had never arrived by mail, as it should have once the chiropractor signed off on my health. I kept checking with the insurance company because I felt responsible to pay the chiropractor as soon as possible.

Finally, the insurance company said, "The check was sent and cashed."

I said, "I never received it."

They said, "Let me check the signature on the back for you."

Imagine my surprise when it was Mark's signature. I felt like I had a rock in my stomach that stayed there all day until Mark came home from work.

"Mark, did you see the check from the insurance company for the chiropractor bill?"

"No, I guess it hasn't come yet."

"They said it did come."

"Well, they must be mistaken."

"They said they have proof it was cashed."

"Really? I hope no one stole it."

"It has your signature on the back."

"That's messed up."

"Mark, I asked for a copy. They faxed it to me. It's your signature."

"Shit. I needed the money for my tires. It's just an insurance company. They have enough money. We pay them every damn month; we deserve it."

"Do you know how long it will take me to pay the chiropractor off without that money?"

"Well, he's got money too. He can wait."

When Mark and I divorced, I agreed to pay off all the bills he had accrued during his multiple affairs and our multiple separations in exchange for him signing over the house to me. After all, he had only lived there for four months, and my father had loaned us the down payment. Even though I had very little money, and I was relying on my father for help, I consolidated his debt (over $5,000 in 1976) and paid off every penny.

Tom and I married after my divorce with Mark was final, and he assisted with paying off the debt incurred in my marriage to Mark. Tom and I made our own mistakes, but at least they were honest mistakes. We borrowed too much money, refinanced our home too many times, financed too many camps and lessons and sports endeavors for our children. We sometimes enabled our children financially by paying off their bad choices and not making them accountable for their own mistakes. But we have paid (and are still paying) every balance we ever borrowed.

Your Story

I heard from teens via YouTube, TED Talks, and personal conversations with past and present students. Teens talked to me about expectations and pressures they feel around money. They see teens become celebrities overnight because of their YouTube channels. They see friends on social media who are constantly posting pictures of their material possessions or the places they've visited. Even as they are dreaming and wishing and comparing, they don't necessarily buy into the whole money glam scene. I contacted several of my past students and asked them if they had anything to share with me about how the money thing has been going since I last saw them in class a few short years ago.

Many of their sentences started with, "I wish," or "Why didn't anyone tell us?" or "Why weren't there classes?" One student reminded me of my teenage self: "Why didn't anyone tell me that just because I could afford the payment on something I wanted didn't make it a good idea to have a payment?" Some shared with me how excited they were when they got their first paycheck—some while they were in high school, and some after high school. While in high school, they often used the money they made for athletic events, prom, school clothes, and supplies. They usually spent everything they made since they still lived with their parents and weren't even thinking about future responsibilities.

I interviewed a short, spunky girl with ginger-colored hair named Morgan who I remembered as a confident, engaged student during high school. "Mrs. J, what's up with us never having any classes about how to handle money?" She shared her story that, once again, sounded a little too much like mine. I wondered if all teens had to learn money lessons the hard way. She spent two years attending community college and working typical young person side jobs. She lived at home and had to use her money for gas and school, so didn't think she had any real financial decisions to make. When she got her first stable job with a pretty reasonable paycheck, she moved out with a friend. The first thing she did was make a list of items she "needed" for her new apartment. She realized that after she paid her portion of the rent and utilities, and bought her groceries and gas, she still had money left over. She bought a TV using one of her new credit cards and decided to get Netflix and Prime since they were only ten bucks each per month.

Fast forward a couple more years. She did well at her job and had received yearly raises. But her car broke down, so she decided to buy a new one. The payment was $400 per month, but she could swing it if she was careful, and another raise would be forthcoming. By the time she was twenty-four, Morgan owed more than she could ever imagine paying back and lived with a boyfriend who also had a $400 car payment and an average-paying job. She had recently filed bankruptcy because she saw no way to get out from under the debt she had accumulated.

Morgan's story is not that different from mine, and not that different from many young people around me who are struggling with money matters. According to Sallie Mae, more than half of college students accumulate $5,000 or more in credit card debt while in school, and one-third owe over $10,000 in credit card debt.

I did meet some teens online who have been successful in money matters. You can meet them too. Look for teen TED Talks and money blogs written by teens. They exist. These teens were taught about money matters by their parents or teachers. They learned to make a budget when their only income was from family members and grandparents who sent checks on birthdays, holidays, and graduations. They created a savings account at a young age and decided how much they would save out of every gift they received. They earned money by babysitting, doing chores, mowing lawns, walking dogs, gardening, pool care, maintenance, house cleaning, car cleaning, running errands. Some teens got retail or fast food jobs. Some came up with do-it-yourself (DIY) jobs like waitressing at a party, tutoring, carrying groceries, teaching a skill. They thought about hours they wasted each week in front of the TV, computer, or on their cell phones and worked to fill those hours in more responsible ways, keeping homework a priority.

These young adults have never had a credit card. They pay for personal expenses like clothes and toiletries themselves. They consider what they need versus what they want. They avoid extras like lattes, tacos, and candy bars and put that money towards their big goals. We are fortunate to be part of the "gig economy" now which means that as teens and adults we can do just about any gig (job) we want. We can be entrepreneurs working out of our homes. We can earn extra money for projects that interest us by using programs like TaskRabbit or GoFundMe.

I was also surprised to see how many sites gave advice to teens and their families that, in my experience, would not have been helpful. Advice like "debt is inevitable," and "credit cards are necessary to build a good credit score," and "large purchases like cars need to be financed," and "no one can attend college without significant student loans," send a message that young people aren't curious, creative, and responsible enough to live a debt-free life. This is not to say that credit cards and student loans are never to be considered. It's only to say that saving from the time we're kids and applying for every scholarship available are two of many options that may save us from the stress caused by debt.

These topics of how and why we spend our money are not

without controversy. Especially when already-successful authors and vloggers provide financial advice that makes it seem easier to become financially stable than it is. It is difficult to find financial success all by ourselves, without the advantage of assistance from family, for example. Financial struggles may have more to do with our earliest financial debts like college loans. Because our parents didn't have the means or didn't make their own best decisions about saving for their children's education, an eighteen-year-old may have to incur debt he or she can't really afford.

In addition, there are many factors like systemic economic problems in our government systems that we did not create. Many of us begin our independence working at minimum-wage jobs or even at jobs that provide an average salary. We cannot begin to compete with the cost of living or the continually-rising cost of attending college or buying a home. When it is right for you, you can become informed about government budgets and possible policy changes at both the state and federal levels, so that you can vote knowledgeably and help make change.

Sometimes I wish money didn't matter so much. I wish it didn't divide people, and offer some people opportunities while neglecting to offer opportunities to others. But during the research and interviews for this chapter, I realized that opening the conversation about money to everyone, no matter their financial background, is the first step in making money matters equal to everyone. Learning about and understanding money is important because having money or not having money affects every decision we make. It affects our stress levels, our relationships, and the potential to be and do everything we want in life.

Top 8 Money Tips

For Teens and Their Parents

Envelopes Choose four or five envelopes and divide any allowance, earnings, gift money you receive between them. Here are some examples:

- Spending (gum, jewelry, movies, gifts, clothes)

- Car (be ready for gas, maintenance, insurance too)

- College

- Savings (unexpected expenses)

- Retirement (If you start saving and investing when you're a teen, you could have over 3 million dollars when you retire!)

- Giving (charities, school fundraisers, church)

Emergency Fund When your savings envelope contains $100, transfer it to a bank savings account, then save some more. Try to get it to $1,000! You may have unexpected expenses, like repairs for a bike, a sick pet, or lost belongings.

Credit Cards Don't use them! Pay with cash! If you feel you must get a credit card in order to establish credit, use a pre-paid card or get a card with a $200 limit. Make sure you completely understand the interest being charged on the card and the consequences of not paying your monthly payments.

Cars Try to save for the entire amount of your first car. Keep an eye on used car prices so that you can see what the lowest possible amount is for a reliable car. Sell that one later, add more savings, and upgrade!

Budget Create a budget and write it down. How much money do you have coming in? Do you have any payments? What is left over? Open savings and checking accounts and then make your own deposits and keep your accounts balanced. (Don't think that if you subtract bills from income that you can spend the "leftover" money. Consider savings, college, retirement and unexpected expenses.)

College	Choose a school that is affordable. Consider going to a community college or an in-state college, working part-time and applying for scholarships and/or student loans. Student loans will go much further if you decide your college budget ahead of time.
Saving	Spend less, save more. If you receive $ for allowance, birthdays, or DIY projects, think of it as "steady income" and put it in your envelopes.
	Look for bargains, second-hand stores, sales, or forego buying anything at all. Think of your bigger goals.
	Spend less on luxury items and experiences. Spend $20 on dinner instead of $30 ($10 for savings).
Investing/ Retirement	Invest as early as you can. When you get your first really good job, listen closely to what the company tells you about savings/retirement options. Some companies will tell you that you can have a deduction taken from your check to be placed in an IRA or Roth or 401(b) or 501(c) (these are all ways to save) and they will match it! That means that if you put in $100 a month, they will also contribute $100 a month. If you do this every month for 20-30 years, you'll have $48,000-$72,000; that's not counting interest earned!! You could be a millionaire!!

What I Wish My Mama Would Have Told Me

I wish my mama would have taught me more explicitly how to be financially responsible. Through my parents' example, I should have learned more than I did. But somehow I didn't. While working in my parents' shoe store when I was in high school, I learned about finances and record keeping. My mother taught me how to keep the incoming and outgoing ledgers current, and how to balance the checkbooks. She taught me that incoming cash minus expenses and savings should always equal zero. I am grateful for these lessons.

When parents are transparent about money and money issues, they set us up for financial success. But somehow I didn't transfer what I learned in the business setting to the reality of my own world of personal finances and the pitfalls that might trip me up.

I wish my mama would have told me about financial planning when I was a teen. It's not easy to think about the long life that is ahead of us when we're teens. But being financially empowered means that we can reach our dream lifestyles. Creating a financial plan as a teenager means looking at one top priority and planning for it now. I wish she would have asked me, "Is the most important thing in life right now to own a car? To go to college? To go to Europe after graduation? Then look at how you spend your money. If someone asks you to go to a movie or go to dinner, it's easier to say no if you have a plan. Don't spend your money on extras if your number one goal is to buy a car."

I wish my mama would have told me that material possessions are just materials. They can be ruined in fires and floods, and other natural disasters. They can be separated between two people in a divorce. I wish my mama would have taken a class with me or read a book with me about living simply and being financially responsible.

Opportunities to Journal

* What messages do you receive about money?
* What have you learned about saving now so you can be financially safe and happy in the future? What changes can you make as a teenager to the way you see and handle money?
* List every way you receive money, including jobs, DIY projects, gifts for birthdays, holidays, etc. Add ideas to expand the ways you can earn your own money even while attending high school.
* Create a budget that shows the money you receive each month, any payment responsibilities you have (even if it's contributing to school events, lunch money, or buying some of your own

clothes), and see how much is left over. What specifically can you do with what is left over?

* What envelopes do you want/need for dividing up your money? Label them and begin today!

Take-Aways

* Every person has the power to be financially responsible.
* Income minus expenses doesn't mean there is room for credit card or car payments. First consider saving for the unexpected, and for future college and retirement responsibilities.
* Be honest, reliable, and diligent with money that has been loaned to you. Pay it back.
* Spend less and save more. An over-abundance of debt may cause an over-abundance of anxiety.
* Ask to budget with your parents, create savings and checking accounts, create an envelope system, avoid credit cards, invest, and plan for your important future.
* Earn your own money. We are a gig economy with many opportunities to be entrepreneurs.
* Don't be fooled by an economy that wants you to spend, use credit cards, and finance everything from a TV to a car.
* Live simply. Material possessions cannot replace peace of mind and financial security.

Chapter 21

Addiction & Alcohol

Do you have a family member who drinks too much? Have you witnessed a gathering get out of hand because people were drunk and became angry or violent? Did you know that a person can also be addicted to sex, gambling, spending, and even overeating? If you haven't seen addiction in your life, maybe you can relate to being addicted to social media, your cell phone, or your partner's affection.

As a teen, and later as an adult, I was addicted to guys who needed me. It was more important to me that I be needed than it was to find someone who had the capacity to be an equal partner. It was more important to me to show my boundless love for someone else than it was for me to love myself. Instead of looking for a healthy partner who loved himself first and challenged himself to be all he could be, I looked for someone who needed me to be the one to love him and challenge him. I didn't know this when I was a teenager, and it's taken me many years to understand my own emotional addictions.

Life is stressful for all of the reasons we've been talking about in this book. There are pressures about everything from body image and social media to sexuality, career choices, and college. As we become involved in serious relationships, there are pressures regarding intimacy, sex, and birth control. We may begin to see red flags, and/or experience fighting, abuse, or violence. Eventually we must support ourselves financially, and the pressures may compound until we feel like we're going to explode . . . or implode.

Either way—whether others see our fear, grief, and anxiety, or we hide it all inside—we may make choices that don't reflect the healthy lifestyle we talked about way back in the beginning of this book. If and when we begin to self-soothe in unhealthy ways with excessive amounts of alcohol, drugs, gambling, sex, food, or spending (or any other addiction we can imagine), we still have the power to change. We can have a safe person to call when we are in need. We can join support groups like AA (Alcoholics Anonymous), or Al-Anon and Alateen (Friends and Family of Alcoholics). You will hear more about these organizations in this chapter. While we do not have any power or control over others in our lives suffering from the diseases of alcoholism or addiction of any kind, we do have the power to change ourselves.

My Story

As a teenager, addiction and alcoholism and all the other "isms" weren't even in my vocabulary. I knew some of my acquaintances drank or took drugs, but none of my close friends did. I didn't even have my first drink until after I married Mark. My parents didn't drink at all. Mark's parents drank a lot. I knew that some of my relatives on my father's side drank a lot too, and I had witnessed family holidays where one or more aunts or uncles had too much to drink, at which point sarcasm turned into biting arguments. I knew that one of my dad's brothers had stopped drinking multiple times, and that his wife wore dark sunglasses that hid black eyes when he abused her after drinking too much. As an adult, I learned that my father's father, who died before I was born, was an angry drunk. I learned that my father's brother contracted esophageal cancer and then liver disease from smoking and drinking. He died from the damage drinking did to his liver.

Because my addiction is to be needed and loved, and to control and fix people, I picked Mark . . . and then I picked Tom. Tom's parents did not drink like Mark's, though, so I thought I was safe there. I hoped the addiction problem would not raise its ugly head in our home. But Tom's family held secrets about relatives who drank too much even to the point of drinking themselves to death. Alcoholism is hereditary, and our three sons inherited alcoholism genes from both sides of their ancestry. Alcoholism is a disease. Just like cancer, diabetes, or any other disease, sometimes it isn't apparent for many years.

Tom eventually adopted Mark's son, and we had two more sons together. Life in a second marriage with three boys brought some problems. There were many more fights—some fair and some not so fair—about money, discipline, chores, responsibilities, school, grades, and all the other arguments that come with raising a family.

Twenty years into our marriage, Tom injured his back on the job. We hung in there through two back surgeries and lots of rehabilitation. Post-injury, he could no longer do the same kind of work, so he returned to school to receive a master's degree in counseling. He attended study groups with young, tight-bodied girls, drank too much, and became a different person for a while. The summer after he graduated was especially long and dark. I'd had enough of the drinking, and told him I didn't want all the alcohol around the house. We had three boys, ages ten, sixteen, and nineteen. What kind of message were we sending?

So began the age of secrets. Tom stopped off at the liquor store to pick up a forty-ouncer and drank it on the side of the house before he came in. He stopped off at the corner bar where everybody knew his name. Sometimes after dinner, he would say, "I'm going for a walk," and hours later he would stagger the four blocks home. My addiction of trying to control what I could not caused me to count bottles in the trash can, check his car, check his breath, call friends and hospitals when he was late, stalk him as he sat alone in bars. We were both lost in our own addictions and our own pain. I felt like a teen again, repeating the same unhealthy cycles that I had been stuck in so many years prior. I did not have the understanding or the strength to stop these destructive cycles. We have talked about always having a safe adult or mentor to talk to when things go wrong. Even though I was no longer a teen during these painful years, I had two mentors who saved my life.

The first was a doctor in the emergency room where I took Tom one night after he stumbled home drunk. My life had become unmanageable, and I didn't know what else to do, so I took him to the hospital to be fixed. I had, once again, failed to change my "boyfriend's" behavior, and I wanted a doctor to help me.

The doctor kept him in a hospital room overnight until he sobered up, and then he said to him: "Your drinking is affecting your family. Your children are home alone right now, and your wife had to bring you here to the hospital in the middle of the night. You are in jeopardy of losing your family. Do you understand that?"

"She's over-reacting. She always does."

"From what I'm seeing and hearing, I don't think she's over-reacting. It appears to me you have a drinking problem. There are programs we have through the hospital to help you, and there are AA programs throughout the city."

I can't imagine that most doctors take the time or use up triage rooms to try to help a co-dependent wife and her drunk husband.

The second mentor came to my home the very next day. She was a friend and a pastor who talked to both of us and helped bring the secrets out of the dark. After questioning us about what had been going on in our lives for the last many months, she finally asked Tom, "Are you willing to stop drinking?"

He said, "No. I don't have a problem with drinking."

The end of the conversation went something like this: "Nancy, Tom doesn't think he has a problem. He is comfortable here. I don't see why he would choose to leave, do you?

"No."

"Can you continue to live like you have been living the last several months?"

I shook my head "no" through my tears.

"Nancy, this decision will have to be yours. Do you see that? Tom is not going to make it any easier for you. What is your decision?"

"I don't want him to leave, but if he doesn't leave, I don't think anything is going to change. I want him to stop drinking."

"Tom, will you stop drinking?"

"No."

My pastor said the words I was too afraid to say: "Okay. Tom, you need to spend the rest of today getting your things together and packing them into your truck. Make calls and find a place to stay. Be prepared to leave in the morning."

She came the next morning and talked to our sons. "Your dad is going to move out for a while. Your mom and dad need some time to think and decide what their next steps are going to be. This doesn't mean he is not coming back. It just means that what is happening now is not working anymore, and we need to make space for something different to happen. Your parents love all of you very much, and this decision has nothing to do with anything any of you have done. Your dad has packed his truck and he's going to stay with your uncle until he can find a place. He will be leaving now."

All of us were crying as we stood up and started hugging each other. I took turns with each son. Tom took turns with each son. Our pastor took turns with each son. Tom and I hugged each other and our boys for whatever hope was left for us. I began recovery in an Al-Anon group. I connected to a higher power of my choosing so that I could learn to stop trying to control things beyond my control. My teenage self finally got the help she needed. She finally had the strength to reach out for help and let the scary secrets out.

Did You Know

Secrets

Some secrets are fun like the telephone game we played as children where one person whispered something into the ear of the person next to her, and the secret continued to be passed down a line of friends until the last person had to say the secret out loud—often completely distorted. Some secrets are to protect us from information we don't need to know at a young age.

Some secrets are the kind families never tell, and those are the secrets that can change our lives forever. Some of us have secrets about sexual abuse, alcoholism, sex addiction, gambling, or overeating. Some of us have been brave enough to share those secrets in recovery. Some of us are still holding on to the secrets, keeping them tucked tightly away in a compartment of our memory where we think they will do no harm.

Sometimes after we tell our secrets we feel better. Sometimes we feel worse for a while, or for a long time. Then we begin to heal. We hear other people tell secrets that are nearly the same as our secrets, and we realize that we are not alone. Sometimes our secrets are different, but our fears, our insecurities, our desire to be loved are the same.

Your Story

In my years of recovery, I have heard many stories of teenage girls who were affected by their alcoholic fathers and/or mothers. Many were members of Alateen. Sometimes they find they have a problem with alcohol themselves. Rather than focus on just one story, I will honor the anonymity of those teens by sharing some excerpts from several of their stories.

In a brochure called *Al-Anon Faces Alcoholism*, one girl shared how it feels to live with two people inside the same mother. She shared the questions that she woke up with each morning:

"Who is going to walk through the door? Is it the disease of alcoholism, or is it the person I love? Will I have to call 911 again tonight? Will I hear the comforting words of a loving mother, or the biting diatribe of a cruel alcoholic?" (See **Resources**.)

She described the emotional roller coaster, the feelings of loneliness, and the constant fear about what would happen next.

Another girl in the same brochure shared, "I kept my room clean, got good grades in school, and never got into trouble. I felt responsible for so many things." She believed that if she were perfect, and took care of everything on her own, both in her personal life and her home life, her parent(s) would not need to drink. (See **Resources**.)

One Alateen brochure called *Alateens Share with Adults in Their Lives* includes letters from teens to their parents:

"I was afraid to tell you how much the drinking and fighting bothered me. I thought constantly about what was going on at home. It got in the way of my schoolwork and friendships. I was so embarrassed that I was afraid to bring my friends over, and at times I didn't even want to go home myself. I felt it was *my* fault we had so many problems."

"Mom, during Dad's early sobriety, you were often too involved with him, and it seemed you didn't care about me. Your arguments made me feel lonely and scared. I tried to get you to stop and pay more attention to me. When you were tense, you'd snap at me, and I felt lost." (See **Resources**.)

In the book, *How Al-Anon Works for Families and Friends of Alcoholics* (Chapter 18), a teen shared some of her alcoholic father's behaviors:

"He showed up for my parent-teacher conference drunk, ran over my bike with the car, kicked me out of the house twice because I was 'ungrateful,' and once, while my mom was out grocery shopping, he locked me in a crawl space and pushed a bookcase in front of the door." Her mother's way of coping was that she sat "in a chair in the corner of the living room, read books, and ate chocolate bars." (See **Resources**.)

In Chapter 13 of the same book, a girl shared about her

experience after her alcoholic dad received a DUI (Driving Under the Influence).

"I took up heavy drinking, and soon afterward I joined the 'sexual revolution' . . . Sex and drinking were the two ways I found to assert my independence and be 'cool.' They were also the very best ways to thoroughly disgust my parents." She ended up pregnant at fourteen. She eventually found her way to AA and Alateen. (See **Resources**.)

In the next chapter, we'll look at how to set boundaries that can help stop secrets and combat patterns of addiction like the ones these young women struggled against.

What I Wish My Mama Would Have Told Me

I wish my mama would have told me that alcoholism runs in families and is a disease. Just like cancer, alcoholism is not a choice. I wish she would have explained to me that in my family of origin I had a fifty-fifty chance of being an alcoholic. My mother's family showed no signs of alcoholism, but my father's side was riddled with secrets about my drunken grandfather, my abusive uncle, beatings, suicides, alcohol-related disease, and even death. I wish she would have explained that my future husband's alcohol-laced DNA mixed with mine would lead to a statistical cocktail that could hurt me or my children in ways I couldn't even begin to imagine.

I wish my mama would have told me that if I'm having trouble with alcohol myself or see a friend having trouble with alcohol, I can seek help. I wish she would have told me that programs like Alateen, Al-Anon, and Alcoholics Anonymous existed. I wish my mama would have helped me decipher red flags that warned me about addiction and how it could affect my life.

Our mamas can't watch our every move nor be by our side when we have our first drink—and it's likely we *will* have that first drink. They can't stop us from making mistakes by berating, embarrassing, or guilting us. I wish she would have loved me through my mistakes and helped me come out the other side stronger and more knowledgeable.

Did You Know

Safety Tips, Anonymity & Support

Safety Tips Choose responsible people to party with if you choose to party. Talk with your friends about safe ways to drink if you are experimenting with alcohol. One person should always be sober.

Never get in a car with a driver who has been drinking. Never drink and drive yourself. If you get that feeling in the pit of your stomach that we've already talked about, listen to the feeling. It could be your guardian angel.

If you don't feel comfortable calling your parents, have another friend or adult that you trust on your calling list.

If you think your drinking is getting out of hand, talk to your parents or an adult you trust and honestly recognize that you love alcohol. You won't be the first one. Trust me on this. There are amazing programs that will save your life.

Anonymity Anonymity literally means honoring people by not naming or identifying them. In AA programs, we know that we keep other people's secrets, whether the secret is their name, their occupation, or any other secret they have voiced. That's usually good. (However, if you believe someone's secret may lead to him/her hurting him/herself or someone else, please tell someone you trust.) Keeping your own secrets can be harmful and unhealthy. That's bad.

Support Alcoholics Anonymous (AA), for those who think they may have a problem with alcohol.

Al-Anon, for friends and families of alcoholics.

Alateen, specifically for teens to help them deal with alcoholism in a family member or friend (see **Resources**).

Opportunities to Journal

✽ Have you ever kept a secret about your own drinking or a friend's drinking because you didn't want to get in trouble? Describe what happened.

✽ Have you ever lost a friend to a drinking incident? What did you learn?

✽ When you read the teen stories, was there one you could relate to? Why?

Take-Aways

✽ Life is stressful, and sometimes you may make unhealthy choices about how to feel better. Unhealthy ways to self-sooth include drinking alcohol, taking drugs, eating, spending, gambling, and/or engaging in sexual behaviors.

✽ Alcoholism is hereditary. It's important to know your family histories and watch for signs that you might have a problem with alcoholism or addiction.

✽ Alcoholism is a disease. Just like cancer or diabetes, sometimes it isn't apparent for many years.

✽ Secrets often put you in harm's way. It's important to have mentors so you can bring your secrets into the light.

✽ Have a safe person to call if you or a friend is drunk and you need a ride home. Be ready to tell someone if you are worried about yourself or a friend.

✽ Alateen is a group especially for teens to help you deal with alcoholism in a friend or family member.

✽ There are many *anonymous* organizations like AA, Al-Anon, and Alateen to help you. *Anonymity* protects secrets and the brave people who tell them (see **Resources**).

Chapter 22

Setting Boundaries

You know those bold, white lines around a soccer field or a football field? Those lines are boundaries that tell the players when they are going out of bounds and the play won't count. Have you seen the fences around cliffs and canyons and pools? Those fences are boundaries that keep us safe. How about the "No Trespassing" signs that protect the boundaries of real estate property? These physical boundaries are easy to picture. Personal boundaries may be harder to picture. While they protect us, they are invisible and different for each person. Boundaries are limits we set in relationships that allow us to protect ourselves. They let those around us know what is acceptable and not acceptable to us. They come from our values and our self-worth.

Personal boundaries do not set expectations on someone else ("You can't..."); they set expectations on *ourselves* not to accept anything less than we desire and deserve ("I won't..."). We never have to allow someone else to pressure, manipulate, or change our boundaries. We can stick to our boundaries, no matter the reaction of the other person. We honor ourselves when we learn to set boundaries that protect our bodies, our self-esteem, our rights, our self-respect, and our power.

My Story

When I was a teenager, I didn't even know what boundaries were. I know now, looking back, that I didn't have boundaries in my relationship with Mark. I know now that when Mark continually had unrealistic expectations of me, counted on me to help him with his homework or be available, dumped on me, asked me to clean up messes or lie for him, caused me anxiety or stress, he was not respecting me. I can't say that he wasn't respecting my boundaries, though. Because I didn't have any.

Truth was, I didn't know I was supposed to. The responsibility was mine to set the boundaries. I could have said no whenever I wanted. I could have protected myself better. Now I know that I didn't have the power to save Mark from his drinking and his other addictions. I only had the power to make and keep boundaries to protect myself, like, "I will decide when and where I have sex." Many years into the future, I didn't have the power to save Tom from his drinking. With the help of my mentors and my recovery programs, I was able to set a boundary to protect myself and my family: "If you choose to drink, you will have to leave."

I learned about boundaries after I finally got to Al-Anon. My job over the next several years was to learn how to set boundaries in my relationships to keep myself safe and sane. When I first went to Al-Anon, I was hurt, overwhelmed, and physically and mentally drained. The fact that I had never learned to set boundaries was my issue. And I had to get better all on my own. A boundary doesn't place expectations on the friend, sibling, spouse, or family member that has hurt us or is sucking out our energy. A boundary does draw a line or circle—I like to imagine a hula hoop—around us to provide protection.

Instead of having boundaries, I allowed myself to cover up for Mark when he called in sick, allowed him to have affair after affair with no consequences, and fixed mistakes caused by his lying and manipulation. Later, I repeated many of these habits with my oldest son. I paid parking tickets, fines, and DMV charges. I paid late rent, late bills, and late late fees. I interfered when I paid for his car repairs, car insurance, and car payments. I didn't honor his personal struggle. I didn't allow him to find his own bottom so that he might seek his own recovery. I bailed him out of financial crisis after financial crisis. I continually said I would not save him the next time because he wasn't paying me back and he wasn't learning from his mistakes. He didn't pay me back. He didn't learn. And yet I saved him again. *I* didn't learn. I didn't set boundaries to protect myself.

The hardest part about boundaries was sticking to my decisions. I had to go one step further than learning *how* to set boundaries. I had to learn how to *keep* them. For me that meant I had to visualize what I was going to say to the person. Sometimes I wrote it down and practiced, or even made up a contract for us to sign. I also had to visualize what could go wrong in that conversation. I visualized everything that person could say to make me change my mind or make me feel guilty or intimidate me into submission or compliance. I was often unsuccessful because of the final part of setting boundaries: "Set them and walk away." We are not in charge of how someone reacts to our boundaries. Whether they scream, manipulate, or buy us flowers, we can stick to the boundary that we know will best protect us.

Do. Not. Argue. With. The. Person. I set multiple boundaries that I honestly and firmly communicated to people in my life who were hurting me emotionally and financially. I then allowed the persons to argue with me, berate me, cuss at me, intimidate me, and knock me out with the "you-owe-me-because-I'm-family-and-you're-supposed-to-love-me" punch. Their behavior was disrespectful, rude, and absolutely not loving . . . and yet I continued to love them. It's okay to continue to love someone for whom we are setting boundaries, but we must learn to detach from them and make our health the most important factor. I continued to learn to take care of myself, and eventually to forgive them and myself.

Did You Know

Setting Your Personal Boundaries

B   **Be** clear on what your values are no matter what others think.

O   **Own** your decisions; no one else can make decisions for you.

U   **Use** as few words as possible and take full responsibility for your boundaries without apology.

N   **Notice** when you're feeling uncomfortable because someone is not respecting your physical or emotional space.

D   **Don't** justify, get angry, or feel guilty for the boundaries you are setting.

A   **Assert** your yes's and no's confidently and truthfully.

R   **Recognize** how your boundaries have been crossed.

I   **Identify** your needs, thoughts, feelings and desires. Protect and pursue them.

E   **Empower** yourself to make healthy choices that are best for YOU!!

S   **Set** your personal boundaries and clearly communicate them no matter the consequences.

Did You Know / Important Facts

What is a Boundary and What Kind of Boundaries Can You Set?

Setting a boundary means you take specific action to change your relationship with an important person in your life. A boundary helps keep you safe, confident and comfortable about yourself and your decision.

Personal Whether you allow a person to criticize you, humiliate you, or talk down to you.

How/when you allow someone to show affection (hug, handshake, kiss, etc.).

Whether you want someone in your personal space.

How much trust you want to give a person.

Social How much time you want to spend with friends/bf/gf.

How often you want to "check in" with friends/bf/gf.

Technological How often you want to be on social media and what you want to share/post about.

How often/what time you want to talk on the phone.

How you want to protect your personal information, including pictures.

Sexual When you want to become more intimate.

Whether you want to change your mind or say no.

What you want to do and when you want to do it.

Mutual understanding and respect of limitations and desires.

Emotional How often you want to communicate with someone and how much personal information you want to share.

What your limits are.

How you protect yourself when someone criticizes, belittles, or invalidates your feelings.

A strange thing happened to me while I was researching this chapter on boundaries. The teen girl inside of me became overwhelmed with all of the mistakes she had made when she was sixteen and seventeen and eighteen. At first she was angry and resentful. Then she was sad and hurt. Then she began to cry. Well, I began to cry. I had an overwhelming sense that I had never dealt with my lack of boundaries during or after my relationship with Mark. I had pretended that my teenage years with Mark were not that bad. I pretended that I had a normal relationship that just didn't work out. But it was not a normal relationship, and I did not have the knowledge or the power to do anything about it.

I decided that I would honor that teen girl inside of me. I decided that I would interview my teen self. I decided that I would give her the opportunity to really feel what happened to her during those years when she did not know how to protect herself. It was like she was on the edge of a windy cliff with no fence around it, no boundary of any kind. She knew that if she stayed one minute longer, she would be pushed over the edge. And yet she stayed.

We will call my "teen self" Mae. That's my middle name. I want to give Mae the power of her very own story. This is a story I have never told anyone. It is a story that has been pushed far into my subconscious. The friend and mentor that I told the story to this morning—nearly fifty years after it happened—said that trauma from our childhood or youth is often stored deep, deep inside us where we hide it because we think it will not do us any harm there. And yet, what happens instead is that the secret stifles our ability to live a complete, joyful, powerful life because it takes energy and pain for it to stay there. We can't learn from what happened because we don't even have access to what happened.

As you know, Mae met Mark when she was sixteen. Mae told me about honeymoon periods of lovely moments: dates and drives and meals and church outings and warm kisses. She told me about periods of time that didn't feel so good: fights and disagreements and angry words and battles about whether or not to have sex. She acknowledged that she had no boundaries. She didn't even know what they were. She always gave in, and she always tried to make Mark feel better. Her well-being was of no concern to her, nor did she feel the danger that came when she hung out too close to the cliff.

Mae had no boundaries over her own body. She allowed Mark to reach up under her skirt in a movie theater, even though people sat on either side of them. She didn't wear underwear when they went to a park or for a walk so that when they sat cross-legged in the grass, he could slip his fingers wherever he wanted to. She let him buy her a bra that clasped in the front so he could easily unclip it whenever he wanted. She allowed him to have sex with her in a crowded restaurant parking lot with cars on both sides. Even though she met the eyes of someone looking in, she didn't make him stop.

Mae had no boundaries over what he could ask of her. She gave up her friends to devote her every moment to him. At school, she made out with him in his car and in the hallways between classes even though she felt embarrassed that people were watching. Mark was proud, so she wanted to please him in front of his friends. She fondled him under a blanket in the same room where her parents sat watching TV. When he convinced her that he may not have the capability to have sex, she proved to him that he could. She came home afterwards to sit with her parents in their living room, her underwear damp with the loss of her virginity.

Eighteen-year-old Mae had no boundaries about how a husband should treat his wife or how he should behave in public. She went camping with him and his car club friends where they all drank themselves into a stupor—or in Mark's case, into a rage. She escaped into their small tent, lying awake listening to his angry voice outside the tent. She heard screaming and yelling, but stayed inside the safe, dark canvas. She found out the next morning that Mark almost killed a guy with his bare hands. It took four guys to get him off the other man. She heard everything and stored it far, far away. She never told anyone. Another time Mark drank too much but drove home anyway. When she tried to stop him, he slammed her head into the steering wheel, and she got a bloody nose. She never told anyone.

Mae had no boundaries about how Mark should treat her family. Mark went with Mae's sixteen-year-old sister, Katie, and Katie's boyfriend, Don (who drove them in his truck), and her fourteen-year-old sister, Jenny, to the beach. On the drive home, Mark and Jenny rode in the back of the truck. Mark was twenty-two and put his hand on fourteen-year-old Jenny's bare leg. Jenny didn't know what to think and pretended she was asleep. Later, Mark told Don that he had "come on" to Jenny and she liked it. Jenny was shocked, but was too afraid to tell. When Mae's dad gave Mark a job in his business, she knew that he and another co-worker were acting inappropriately when her father wasn't there—creating sexual contests that they would take home to their wives, and taking long lunch breaks to go home and have sex—but she said nothing.

Mae had no boundaries about how many times she would allow Mark to cheat on her. After his first affair, she was grateful he came home. He said she was the only girl he ever loved. She didn't say one thing about the affair. She didn't set one boundary to protect herself from any future breaches. She took him back, tried to make herself more sexy and beautiful, and became willing to try sexual acts that made her uncomfortable. Maybe if she became more appealing, he wouldn't cheat again. She believed it was her fault, not his. After his second affair, she was grateful Mark came home. He said she was the only girl he ever loved.

Mae had no boundaries over her own body when she was pregnant. Mark's third affair started during the last trimester of her pregnancy.

She thought it was because she wasn't skinny enough, sexy enough, beautiful enough. The new woman was ten years older than her with two children. Mae thought Mark's latest affair partner must be more interesting, more knowledgeable, more sexual than her. She never complained during her pregnancy. Mae made sure she never acted tired or sick or unwilling to have sex under any circumstances.

Mae had no boundaries for how a husband and father should care for her and his new baby when they returned home from the hospital. Mark didn't apologize for the affair this time, but he promised his parents that he would come back home after his son was born. He said that Mae was still the only girl for him. Mae was determined to keep him this time. He wanted to have sex immediately after the baby was born. When most women would have been too sore from childbirth and heavy bleeding, she complied. He wanted to show her the tricks he had learned during his last affair, as if she would appreciate his effort.

It was summer time; they'd had a June baby. Mae only gained fifteen pounds during her pregnancy, so she lost the weight quickly. She wore skimpy bikinis that showed off her flat stomach and nursing breasts. She tried to be the perfect wife and mother. She never asked anything of Mark, including taking care of his son. He stayed for four months.

Your Story

Maybe after reading Mae's story, there are some scenarios that sound familiar to you. Maybe you have been in a situation where you didn't protect your body or allowed someone else to ask more from you than you were willing to give. Maybe you've seen an older sister or even your mother mistreated or disrespected in private or public. Maybe you've worried about a younger sibling or family member because of an abusive person in your life. Maybe you've experienced a partner cheating on you or have watched someone you love being taken advantage of in some way. Some things don't change from generation to generation.

Teens today, though, have additional concerns for which they may have to set boundaries that Mae never had to consider. There are many situations that can arise because of modern technology, social media, and cell phones. Sexting, for example, may be something to enjoy in a committed relationship, or it may be something that you are not ready for or interested in. Either way, it's good to know the risks. For example, I interviewed sixteen-year-old Amy, who had shared both sexting and semi-nude photos with her boyfriend during their nine-month relationship. They had a pretty ugly break-up after he started a side relationship without her knowledge. He thought she was being unreasonable to break up after one mistake. After trying to get her back and failing, he shared some of the sexting and semi-nude photos on his social media site. Amy was devastated and embarrassed. I asked her whether at any point during the sexting or picture-taking, her intuition had tried to caution her. She said, "I was always nervous about both sexting and having my boyfriend take semi-nude pictures, but I knew he liked it, and I wanted to please him." Amy ignored her intuition—like I did many times when I was a teen—and in retrospect wished she had set a boundary to protect herself early on. It's always harder to set boundaries when the relationship is eight or nine months old than when the relationship is brand new.

Like making a wish list of all the character traits you want in a healthy relationship (**Chapter 6**) or being aware of everything that can go wrong when using social media, cell phones, or technology of any kind (**Chapter 4**), it's good to decide on some boundaries early on in your teenage life. The list may be easier to compile before you enter into a relationship, but it's never too late to stop and start over. I even set a new list of boundaries for myself while writing this chapter.

Chapters 12 and 13 talk about stages of intimacy and decisions before having sex. You can choose how far you want to go sexually long before you are in the middle of a passionate moment. You can choose whether you want to give a guy a blow job even though he's pressuring you, arguing that blow jobs are not real sex. You can choose whether you want to set boundaries about your body, what a partner can ask of you and expect of you, like Mae wished she would have done. You can set boundaries about whether you want to sext, share photos, or have an exclusive relationship like Amy wished she would have done. Whether you are a person who has already set good boundaries or someone who is still learning to set boundaries, it's never too late to make your own body the most important body in your life.

What I Wish My Mama Would Have Told Me

I wish my mama would have taught me about boundaries. I wish she would have warned me that society and culture sometimes set up women to save, mop up after, and please others before ourselves. I wish she would have told me that I did not need people in my life who did not respect my words or my needs or my boundaries. I wish she would have told me that I never had to do anything that made me uncomfortable and that I was the only one who got to decide what to do with my body. I was the only one who got to decide how to keep myself safe. I wish she would have said, "You are good enough and beautiful enough *all by yourself.*"

I wish she would have warned me that sometimes boundaries hurt. I wish she would have told me, "Sometimes the person who hurts you is family. You will grieve. You will think your life is ending. But the only journey you have any control over is your own. Hold compassion in your heart for the person you love or miss. Forgive the person. Send good thoughts out into the universe, and surround the person with well wishes. There is a possibility that person will seek recovery or will learn from the strong boundary you bravely set. You will have a choice whether to make that person a part of your life again. Be cautious. You are the most important person to consider. Love yourself deeply."

Opportunities to Journal

* Do you have any friends that ask you to lie for them or "cover up" for them? If so, how does that make you feel? What are you getting out of that relationship?

* Describe a time when a friend called you too late or too many times each day or constantly checked up on you. How would you set a boundary for that friend?

* Think of a friend who makes you feel uncomfortable. Why do you feel that way? List three things that you would like that friend to stop doing around you. How can you communicate your feelings to the friend?

* Are you involved with a partner who is asking for more physically than you are comfortable giving? Write down the boundary that you wish to set to protect your body. What will you say and how will you stick to it?

* Write a script of what you will say next time you feel your boundaries are not respected by a family member, close friend, or significant other.

Take-Aways

* Boundaries keep you safe. They let those around you know what is acceptable and not acceptable to you.

* A boundary doesn't set expectations on someone else; it sets expectations on *you* not to accept anything less than you desire and deserve.

* Allowing someone to lie, manipulate, and change your boundaries doesn't help them or you.

* After you set a boundary, you must stick to it, no matter the reaction of the other person.

* Following the B-O-U-N-D-A-R-I-E-S acrostic will keep you strong and healthy.

* There are personal, social, technological, sexual, and emotional boundaries that can help you protect yourself.

* Honor yourself by learning to set boundaries that protect your body, your self-esteem, your rights, your self-respect, and your power.

Chapter 23

Self-Care

My teen self didn't start speaking to me until this book was almost finished. There were a lot of stories that she held for me in the deepest corners of my subconscious, and I think she felt relieved to finally bring some of her secrets out into the light. If you are reading this while you are still a teen, you have the opportunity to think about your stressors and also about how strong, beautiful, and important you are. You have the opportunity to take care of yourself and bring everything into the light *now* so you can find joy and power *now* in your teenage years. If you are reading this while you are an adult, I encourage you to seek out your teen self and help her to integrate with who you are today.

Self-care is such an important part of living a full and complete life. It's not just bubble baths, candles, and soft music. It's definitely not about who likes us and who doesn't, or whether we received compliments on our latest outfit. It's not about whether we are feeling special or loved by a boy or girl or even a group of people. Sometimes self-care is hard. In our darkest moments, it might be about taking a shower, putting on our favorite T-shirt and jeans, and going for a walk. In our best moments, we still need to care for ourselves first, before anyone else.

My Story

Here we are almost at the end of this book, and you know my teenage self pretty well by now. She didn't take care of herself as well as she could have in high school. She didn't listen to her intuition and she didn't see the red flags waving all around her. She knew nothing about birth control, intimacy, abuse, or violence. She collected the stress of fighting, money matters, addiction, and abandonment, and she stuffed them deep inside herself.

I don't know at what point my teenage self got so far off track. I called this book, *Things My Mama Never Told Me* because there really are many things I wish my mama would have told me. But the bottom line is that my mother and father did the best they could to raise me, and they gave me many gifts that have made me who I am today. They were supportive and loving. They gave me multiple opportunities to learn, to travel, to experience music and dance, to search for spirituality, and to give back to my community.

I had safe opportunities to hang out with boys in my church group where I kissed my first boyfriend in the eighth grade. I watched my favorite shows on TV, experimented with makeup my mother bought me, tried different hairstyles, made money at my first job in a pizza parlor, sewed and bought my own clothes, and drove the family Chevrolet when I got my license at sixteen. I got good grades and kept busy. I took bubble baths, read, and played the piano. It seems that I should have had the social, mental, and spiritual capacity to protect myself and know my self-worth. And yet somehow my brains leaked out of my heart when I fell in love. The lessons I finally learned (and am still learning) about how to love myself more than any other person I will ever meet are the lessons that inspired me to think about what my mama didn't tell me . . . and then to tell you.

After my minister helped me set a boundary to protect myself and my sons from the influence of Tom's drinking, I learned to take better care of myself. At first, without my constant interference, Tom drank more. His drinking strained his interactions with us, but also strained his work relationships. He missed us and bargained to come home. "If I drink less or only drink on weekends or only drink on holidays . . . then can I come home?" I protected myself and my sons with a boundary asking for ninety AA meetings in ninety days. Absolute sobriety. My sons and I applauded tokens received for thirty days of sobriety, sixty days, and then ninety days. Our family was reunited after a long summer of change and growth.

While Tom worked his program, I worked mine. I got my very own Al-Anon sponsor who began to teach me some of the lessons I had either not received or had ignored. She taught me how to take care of myself. I began to heal. And today I am helping my teenage self to heal. My sponsor said, "Keep your life simple. Surround your children and grandchildren with love and compassion—wherever they are in their journey. Maybe their teen selves are hurting as well." She taught me to take responsibility for my part in my life's decisions. She taught me to be gentle with myself. She told me to imagine being warmed by love from some power greater than myself. She said the power could be anything I wanted it to be: the wind, clouds, nature, energy, spirit, or an actual physical being.

I began to take care of myself by gardening, reading, listening to music, hanging out with friends and family, or going for a long walk. I was able to find some serenity. I began to forgive myself. I forgave my beautiful, loving mama and took responsibility for my teen self and my grown-up self.

Tips for Self-Care

S **Sleep**, eat and exercise. Eat the right foods in the right quantities. Sleep more. Move a little each day, even if exercise is not really your thing. Walk a dog. Sign up for a 5K in the park. Join a dance class.

E **Engage** with your imagination. Write, draw, journal, paint. Check out local community centers for free classes. Try a new hobby or discover a new passion. Go to the library and check out a book or a movie. Listen to podcasts.

L **Love** yourself. Say affirmations like "I love and appreciate you," "You're beautiful," "You are worthy and deserve greatness," "You are the most important person in my life." Take a break from school, homework, extracurricular activities, your job and any other stressors when you need to. Take a long shower, paint your nails, style your hair, or give yourself a facial. Go for a walk, dance, or sing to the mirror.

F **Find** inspiration. Meditate. Stop and breathe before and after you brush your teeth, or before a test at school, or while listening to music. Explore what spirituality means to you. Attend a religious or spiritual service. Read scripture or inspirational sayings.

C **Connect** with friends, family and those in need. Cook or bake together. FaceTime or Skype with someone. Create a goal together and support each other in reaching it. Walk dogs at an animal shelter. Tutor kids younger than you. Raise money for a cause. Help out with a political campaign. Do something for someone else and make yourself happier too.

A **Adopt** a schedule. Make professional self-care appointments when needed. Do your homework so you don't fall behind. Clean your room and do your chores. Attend to important tasks. Plan your financial life. Schedule your self-care!

R **Release** emotions. Watch a sad/funny movie or episode. Talk to a spiritual leader or therapist. Sing at the top of your lungs. Scream into your pillow. Caress your own body.

E **Enjoy** nature. Take a walk or go on a hike. Grow some vegetables or plant a window box. Visit a garden center or a nursery. Go outside; leave your phone behind. Do outdoor social events instead of social media. Rather than mindlessly surfing the net, body surf at the beach.

Your Story

At the end of every interview with a teenager, I asked, "What do you do to take care of yourself?" I've shared bits and pieces of their suggestions in other places, but they bear repeating:

Isabel told me, "I surround myself with people who love me and understand me. I try to remember that stress is temporary, but the results of my hard work and reaching my goals will bring me satisfaction and happiness."

Rosalie said, "Cleaning and organizing calms me. I hug my dog and listen to music. I talk to Ms. Hohenstein, my teacher and academy director. I find ways to participate in and be proud of my culture."

Jessica said, "I walk my dogs and play with my two-year-old brother. I try to approach stress differently by writing it down, getting it out of my head. My friends and I hang out sometimes and check in on each other. We compliment each other. Sometimes I write the bad stressors down and then crumple up the paper. I tried to help one friend who stayed in bed watching Netflix because she felt depressed. We were far away from each other and weren't telling each other how we really were feeling. It's easy to just ask each other, 'How are you feeling?'"

Roxanne told me that she says the affirmation, "I can do it." She said, "Then I can manage all the feelings I am experiencing. I have an inner strength that tells me I can do it. I look for positive people, and radiate positivity and strength. I don't want anyone else to have negative feelings. I want to protect everyone around me. I want them to forget about their problems, not to ever have to go through what I have gone through. I am a gift. Life is not a disadvantage. I will just work harder. I can work twice as hard as anyone else."

Mae finally realized that setting boundaries to protect herself was a sign of good self-care, but also represented self-respect. Communicating her needs during the relationship with her boyfriend and setting limits that protected her would have been far more important than the relationship itself. Honoring the relationships she already had with her girlfriends and family members would have been a positive choice and may have been able to influence her once the red flags started stabbing her in the eye.

If we don't know how to take care of ourselves perfectly all the time, or we choose not to take care of ourselves perfectly all the time, there's nothing wrong with us. Bad habits are hard to break, and good habits take lots of practice. We can try a few ways to take care of ourselves that we already know make us feel better like eating right, exercising, sleeping enough, and unplugging now and then. We can also try some new options from the self-care chart like volunteering, meditating, or trying a new hobby that brings us inspiration.

We have talked a lot about how difficult self-care can be, especially for a teen. We have talked about some of the positive outcomes of good self-care. My friend, Cristina, reminded me of an important word I want to end this chapter with: "Autonomy." Autonomy means "the right or condition of *self-government.*" This word is so important for us when we're teens or when we're healing our teen selves, because we are the only ones who can *govern* us. I can make independent decisions that protect me. I do not ever have to live under the influence of what any other person thinks is right for me. Autonomy means I am a thinker. I am empowered. I can live by the idea that I will care for myself first, no matter what my friends or enemies or parents or social media think is best for me. I think of my autonomous self as my body, mind, and spirit.

Circle of Care

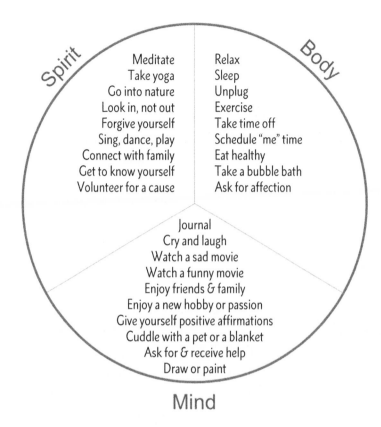

Spirit

Meditate
Take yoga
Go into nature
Look in, not out
Forgive yourself
Sing, dance, play
Connect with family
Get to know yourself
Volunteer for a cause

Body

Relax
Sleep
Unplug
Exercise
Take time off
Schedule "me" time
Eat healthy
Take a bubble bath
Ask for affection

Journal
Cry and laugh
Watch a sad movie
Watch a funny movie
Enjoy friends & family
Enjoy a new hobby or passion
Give yourself positive affirmations
Cuddle with a pet or a blanket
Ask for & receive help
Draw or paint

Mind

What I Wish My Mama Would Have Told Me

I wish my mama would have told me that taking care of myself was the first, most important thing I could do for myself and all of those around me. If I didn't love myself, no one else would love me either. My mother played cards with her girlfriends, had her hair washed and styled every week, and painted her nails herself. She loved makeup and clothes and jewelry. She sewed, cooked, baked, and painted. Those were just the hobbies she did without my father. I wish she would have told me that all those activities she did with her girlfriends, and with and for herself, were important. They were the ways she took care of herself. I wish she would have told me that she was her own best friend, and she took care of herself because she loved herself.

Opportunities to Journal

* Write about a time when you had an amazing day with your girlfriends. How did that make you feel?
* Write about a time when you did something alone that turned out to be completely fulfilling and healing. How did that make you feel?
* Think about a time when you completed an artistic project, school project, or athletic endeavor that made you proud. Write about the experience.
* What is one small thing you can start doing daily to take care of yourself?

Take-Aways

* You are strong, beautiful, and important.
* Identify your stressors and bring them into the light.
* When you're at your lowest, self-care is the hardest, but is also the most important gift you can give yourself.
* Even in the best of upbringings, teen selves are often traumatized in small and large ways. Accept that you must love yourself more than any other person.
* In the end, you will learn to take responsibility for your part in how your life turns out.
* Tips for self-care teach you to Sleep, eat, and exercise; Engage with your imagination; Love yourself; Find inspiration; Connect with friends, family, and those in need; Adopt a schedule; Release emotions; and Enjoy nature.
* Self-care includes many of the components of previous chapters like developing good communication, setting boundaries to

protect yourself, honoring all of your relationships, and protecting yourself when confronted by red flags.

* It's important for you to find your autonomy by self-governing your body, mind, and spirit. Baby steps will work: Add in one small thing you can do for yourself today.

* You are your own best friend and must love yourself before anyone else.

Chapter 24

Forgiveness

Throughout this book we have heard stories about teens who have been hurt by friends, boyfriends, parents, adults, school systems, and even governments. Some actions can be more easily forgiven, like friends' comments on social media or a boyfriend being insensitive. Some actions, like abuse, addiction, or neglect, may feel impossible to forgive. And that's okay. The purpose of forgiveness is for us, not for the offending person.

The act of forgiveness helps us get rid of negative feelings and thoughts that may continue to upset us long after a person has hurt us. If we can give up feelings of hurt, pain, and revenge and replace them with kindness and compassion, we are the ones who benefit. Forgiveness does not mean we have to forget. Forgiveness is deciding how we will respond to what happened to us. If we respond with resentment and anger, we do not protect our bodies, minds, and hearts from the effects of negative emotion.

Forgiveness does not say that what happened to us was okay. It doesn't change the fact that someone hurt us. Forgiving stops the pain of our pasts from defining our forevers. Forgiveness heals the cracks in our hearts—or at least patches them—and allows us to find peace and happiness again. We can forgive those who hurt us intentionally (like Mark), forgive those who hurt us unintentionally (like my mama), and ultimately forgive ourselves.

My Story

When I was a teen, I don't know that I ever heard anyone say, "Will you forgive me?" Likewise, I never heard anyone say, "You are forgiven." It makes sense to me now that sometimes forgiveness was being talked about even if the "F" word wasn't used. Growing up, if I told my mother about a friend or teacher or acquaintance who had treated me badly, she would usually say, "He/she didn't mean it," or "He/she must have been having a bad day," or "Everyone makes mistakes." I did hear other parents in the neighborhood or out in the world make comments like, "Don't let him walk all over you!" or "If she hits you, hit her back," or "He probably deserved it." As a child and a teen, I received and stored these messages from the adults in my life about how I should handle situations when someone treated me badly. My paternal aunts and uncles frequently fought with each other about something someone said or did to hurt the other person's feelings. They would complain about each other and hold grudges—in some cases until death. My maternal aunts and uncles, on the other hand, acted like nothing had happened rather than communicate their need to give or receive forgiveness.

I can see now that all of these phrases and behaviors instructed me on whether I should forgive someone or not. I preferred my mother's family who ignored discontent over the painful confrontations of my father's family. I learned that I should always be the forgiver, not expecting accountability from the other person, and preferably never even letting them know about it. Others may have learned that the fault lies with someone else, leaving no necessity to forgive or ask for forgiveness. In my relationship with Mark, repeatedly forgiving him for his irresponsible and dishonorable actions gave him the message that he didn't have to change, which left me feeling violated and disrespected.

Even though I didn't understand my part in the dysfunction of my relationship with Mark when I was a teenager, I understand it now. I know now that I should have stood up for myself, stayed engaged with positive friends and family, followed my intuition when I knew that Mark was not a good man for me, and left when all the signs were reading "Danger." But today, if I do not forgive Mark for his part in our unhealthy relationship, I am the one who holds that anger, resentment, and pain inside my body and mind and heart. If I don't forgive, I will remain powerless, staying in the victim mode. I will never heal the pain and move forward with my life. My forgiveness of Mark is not about whether he deserves it; it's about my physical and emotional health. Forgiving Mark is not a one-time event. It continues to be an ongoing process. I had to admit my part in our young relationship. I didn't have to forgive any or all of his actions, but I tried to see his humanity and forgive that. Today, I forgive Mark.

Tom has been sober for twenty-five years. We have been married forty-two years. We have loved, laughed, disagreed, fought, and loved again. We have witnessed our sons' marriages and our grandchildren's births. We have worried about our adult sons as they face their own demons, challenges and accomplishments . . . just like we did. I am grateful for our journey together. Today, I forgive Tom.

Forgiving my sweet mama came easier, especially at the end of the writing process that culminated in this book. She and my father provided me with a safe, loving place in which to grow. She did the very best she could. There were factors far beyond her control in the decisions I made in my own destiny. As I made my own mistakes as a mother, I began to have a deeper, more compassionate understanding of how difficult motherhood is. I knew that I had to forgive my mama for all the things she never told me. Today, I forgive my loving, kind mama.

I began the long and difficult process of forgiving myself. I had to forgive myself for all of the times I didn't teach my sons the lessons they needed to become healthy, honest, compassionate human beings. I had to acknowledge, and then forgive the fact that my sons could also write a book about all the things they wish their mama would have told them. In therapy, I continued to face the pain of my mistakes. As I allowed the pain to exit my heart, I chose to replace it with positive things that I wanted for myself and for my family. I continued to ask for compassion, hope, love, patience, health, sustenance, gratitude, and joy. I have had to forgive myself again and again. I have had to ask my sons and my husband for forgiveness again and again. Today, I forgive myself.

I continue to ask others for help. My friend, Parminder, said, "Say the affirmation, 'Please forgive me. I love you. Thank you. I'm sorry.' Say it every day for thirty days, once for each son, once for your husband, and once for yourself. When I worried that I could never do enough to seek forgiveness from my family, my Al-Anon sponsor said, "Grace comes from your higher power, not from other humans. Humans are not equipped to judge themselves, and judgment is often shame-based and guilt-ridden. Imagine that the same higher power that loves you is pouring endless amounts of love and compassion down on your sons, your husband, and your entire family."

I know now that love is powerful enough to allow me to forgive a person even when I cannot forgive their actions. Love can protect me even when I have no control over how my request for forgiveness is received.

Forgiveness

What Forgiveness Is and Isn't and How and Why to Do It

Forgiveness Is Not	Forgiveness Is	How to Forgive	Why Forgive?
Saying that the offense was okay. It does not condone, minimize, or excuse wrongdoing.	Deciding how you will respond to what happened.	Forgive yourself first; then it will be easier to forgive others.	To live without resentment and gain a better view of yourself.
Changing or controlling anything that happened.	Protecting your body, mind, and heart from resentment, anger, grudges and past mistakes.	Think kindness: it benefits the forgiver more than the forgiven person.	To start the healing process and move forward with your life.
Trying to change the other person.	Healing from a negative event so you can live in peace and good health.	Accept that some things just happen; they are not intentional.	To gain power; otherwise you let the person have power over you by ruining your day, week, life.

Forgiveness Is Not	Forgiveness Is	How to Forgive	Why Forgive?
Expecting the other person to forgive you or apologize for his/her part.	Refocusing your thoughts on positive emotions of understanding, empathy, and compassion towards the person who hurt you even when it's not expected or deserved.	Admit your part and accept responsibility when necessary; then apologize and forgive.	To stop reliving the event that makes us bitter, unhappy, angry, tense, frustrated.
Only given to those we like.	Providing the other person a chance to grow and change.	Separate the action from the person; then forgive the person.	To get out of trauma/victim mode. So our brain will stop releasing survival chemicals.
A one-time process of repairing broken relationships or hearts.	Recognizing that life is messy and unpredictable, that we are all fallible humans capable of messing up.	Say the affirmation to yourself or someone else, "Please forgive me. I love you. Thank you. I'm sorry."	To increase brain activation in five brain regions, increasing positive emotions and academic success.

Your Story

Being a teen is a particularly difficult time in our lives because we often say things we don't mean to others (parents, friends, siblings), and they say things they don't mean in response. In several chapters, we have talked about trying to find balance in our lives. Looking at the behaviors that require forgiveness, we might also benefit from looking for balance. The truth is that our teen selves and everyone surrounding us is somewhere in the middle, sometimes wrong, sometimes right, sometimes doing the wounding and sometimes receiving the wounding. The more we can forgive ourselves and those around us—both those whom we love and those who may be acquaintances or strangers—the more we will be able to forgive ourselves and come out of our teen years with our hearts intact.

In the many interviews I conducted with brave, resilient teens, I heard stories of broken hearts, but I also heard stories of forgiveness.

Roxanne (Chapter 7) on Forgiving Her Mom:

Roxanne shared how resentful she was toward her mother when she did not protect her from her abusive stepfather. Her stepfather would threaten to send her to an orphanage, ignore her, or leave her behind when he drove her siblings to school. When Roxanne told her mother what was going on, her mother didn't stand up for her. She said, "You're just a kid. You can't do anything about it." Roxanne lost all trust in her mom and refused to speak in her own home for several months. In the end, the stepdad left and Roxanne had to choose whether she was going to go on resenting her mom for the time she felt abandoned. Roxanne said, "I don't want to see my life as a disadvantage. I want to see the positivity in each person." She was able to leave the nonsupportive actions of her mother behind and forgive her. She introduced me to her mother with pride and acknowledged that they had been through a lot together: "We work as a team to take care of my younger siblings."

Sara (Chapter 4) on Forgiving Her Boyfriend:

Sara shared how difficult it was to see her relationship with her boyfriend judged on Instagram after they broke up. Her boyfriend posted pictures of people he was hanging out with post-breakup. "He said ugly things about me on his Instagram account." Mutual friends took sides, and even after unfriending him, she continued to hear stories about him and the hurtful comments he was making. In the end, Sara had to accept that "some things just happen; they are not intentional." She had to think kindness for the person—not the actions he took—in order to benefit herself.

Claudia (Chapter 15) on Forgiving Herself:

Claudia had to forgive herself for continuing to stay in a relationship controlled by her boyfriend in every way. He controlled her time, her friends, even her conversations with her teacher (me). He ignored her during the school day if he was angry with her and expected her to have sex with him after the school day ended. By the time she graduated, she was pregnant with his child, and he refused to take any responsibility. She told me when she came back to visit after graduation that she had to forgive herself even more than him because she had shared with me and with her friends a year previously that, "He is too possessive. He's always mad at me and wants to control everything I do. I know he's not good for me." She felt like a failure that she stayed with him even though she knew what he was like. She had to forgive his actions. She knew that if she didn't leave the resentment behind, she and her baby would be victims forever.

Without forgiveness, the heart stays broken:

The "When We **Don't** Forgive" Heart

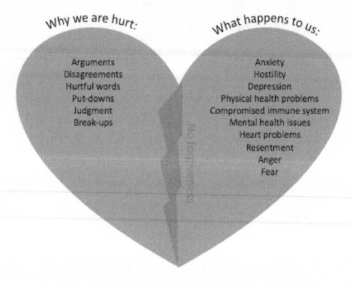

Why we are hurt:

Arguments
Disagreements
Hurtful words
Put-downs
Judgment
Break-ups

What happens to us:

Anxiety
Hostility
Depression
Physical health problems
Compromised immune system
Mental health issues
Heart problems
Resentment
Anger
Fear

With forgiveness, the heart can heal:

The "When We **Do** Forgive" Heart

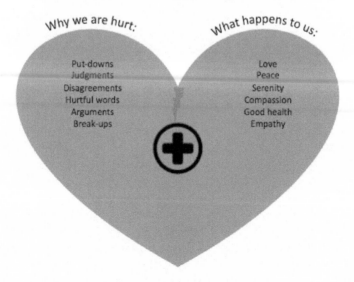

Why we are hurt:

Put-downs
Judgments
Disagreements
Hurtful words
Arguments
Break-ups

What happens to us:

Love
Peace
Serenity
Compassion
Good health
Empathy

What I Wish My Mama Would Have Told Me

I wish my mama would have told me that the best way to survive broken relationships, mistakes, and misunderstandings is to forgive myself and the others in my life again and again and again. I wish she would have told me that forgiveness can be complicated because the person I am trying to forgive may not be in my life anymore. The person I am trying to forgive may have seriously injured or molested me and doesn't deserve my forgiveness. I wish she would have told me that there would be many times in my life where friends or boyfriends or teachers or parents—or any other number of people—would hurt me, sometimes intentionally and sometimes unintentionally.

And finally, I wish she would have told me that, in the end, the person who will be hurt the most by not forgiving would be me. I cannot change the other person. I can only forgive and move on, and hope that in their own time, they will forgive me as well.

In wishing that my mama told me these things about forgiveness, I have to first forgive her for every lesson she didn't teach me, and I have to forgive myself for every lesson she taught me that I didn't listen to. I forgive my dear mama with all of my cracked and healing heart. More importantly, I thank her for the many lessons that she did teach me that allowed me to struggle through my own decisions, take responsibility for them, and return to a healthier path. I am grateful for every lesson she taught me and every lesson I learned through my own mistakes.

Opportunities to Journal

* Have you ever been so mad or frustrated that you couldn't think of anything else? Just thinking of a certain person or event made it hard for you to sleep or eat? What happened, and what did you do about it?

* Have you ever hurt somebody and maybe he/she didn't talk to

you for a long time or he/she broke up with you? What happened? Do you wish that person could have forgiven you? Can you forgive yourself?

* Who do you have in your life that you need to forgive? What can you do about it?

* How does it make you feel when you haven't forgiven someone? Can you forgive the person even if you will never forget what he/she did to you, and even though that person may not be in your life anymore?

* When have you been forgiven though you may not have deserved it?

* Fill the left side of the forgiveness heart with things that hurt you in a relationship. Write about how and why you might be able to forgive the person.

The "When We <u>Do</u> Forgive" Heart

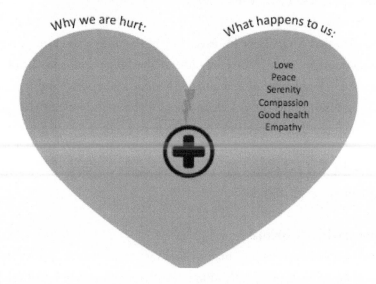

Why we are hurt:

What happens to us:

Love
Peace
Serenity
Compassion
Good health
Empathy

Take-Aways

* Forgiveness helps you get rid of negative feelings so you can heal.

* Forgiveness does not mean that you forget or condone the act that needs forgiving.

* Teens receive messages from adults and media of all types that tell them whether to forgive or not.

* Sometimes you're wrong, and sometimes a family member or friend is wrong. Look for balance, understanding, and compassion.

* When you don't forgive those who hurt you, you end up with broken hearts full of resentment, anger, fear, depression, and possibly physical or mental problems.

* When you can forgive even serious actions against you, you find healing and develop personal strength.

* The best way to survive broken relationships, mistakes, and misunderstandings is to forgive yourself again and again and again.

Chapter 25

Your Brave Tomorrow

Phew! Thanks for sticking with me through twenty-four chapters of information, advice, and stories. I hope you have had opportunities to reflect, grow, learn, and maybe open your eyes to a new perspective or two. By sharing this time with me, you honored my teen self and my adult self. You honored the amazing, brave teens who shared difficult stories and secrets so that your life might be more fulfilling, and you honored yourselves.

I hope you continue to let the stories move in and out of your heart and your consciousness. Don't be concerned with all of the research and facts. There will be no quiz, and facts are always there for you to refer back to in the future. Take what you like, and leave the rest.

If you really need a particular story right now, let it enter your heart completely and start to heal what was broken. If you haven't experienced a story yet, store the knowledge and lessons in your creative brain so that you will recognize the emotions when they arise later.

You will make your own mistakes. You will bravely challenge your own opponents. You will confront your own stereotypes, prejudices, and unrealistic expectations. You will suffer the effects of stress and poor choices. Don't be afraid. You will survive. You are strong and powerful.

What I Hope for You

In the end, I hope that you will take away from this experience some new tools and perhaps a few new ideals. I hope that you will choose your own look and see yourself as different and beautiful. I hope you will be a supportive friend to yourself first, and then maybe to another girl, someone being bullied, or even the bully. I hope you carry yourself with pride and confidence. I hope you take control of your technology time and your personal face-to-face time. I hope you surround yourself with positivity and healthy habits. I hope you pursue creativity and choose a career that you are passionate about. I hope you listen to your intuition, opt out when something doesn't feel right, and run, sweet girl, run when you need to protect yourself. I hope you choose a healthy partner when and if you're ready for a partner. I hope you begin to make decisions that define your personal power, your comfort with intimacy, and your boundaries. I hope you will have some tools and facts at your disposal to protect you from STDs, unwanted pregnancy, abuse, violence, and addiction. I hope you have acquired some strategies to fight fair and manage money. I hope that you will take care of yourself and forgive yourself when you don't do some of these things perfectly . . . because you won't.

What I Want for You

No matter how many mistakes you make along the way, I want you to forgive yourself. (It's unlikely you will make more mistakes than me and my incredible teen storytellers!) I want you to empower yourself and honor yourself. I want you to make healthy decisions that are best for you. I want you to keep your life simple and love yourself. And when you think you haven't done one dang thing right, I want you to remember that you get as many do-overs as you need. When you are overwhelmed and depressed, I want you to remember the stories my teen students and friends have shared. I want you to take extra special good care of yourself. I want you to make sure that your body, mind, and spirit are receiving love, sustenance, spirituality, and acceptance. *I want you to care for your body* by relaxing, sleeping, exercising, and eating healthy. *I want you to care for your mind* by laughing and crying; enjoying friends, family, hobbies, and passions; giving yourself positive affirmations; asking for and receiving help and affection. *I want you to care for your spirit* by meditating, taking yoga, singing, dancing, playing, going out into nature, forgiving yourself and getting to know yourself. If you are having a hard time taking care of yourself, I want you to seek help from an adult you care about, a therapist, or a helpline. You matter to me.

Call to Action

Will you pick one small step to take today? Promise me you'll do something for yourself. I'm inserting the Self-Care chart here again. Will you circle one thing in one category that you will do tomorrow? The next day or week or two, try a new category, and do one more thing. You don't have to change overnight, and you don't have to pinky swear that after you try something once, you will do it for the rest of your life. Trust me. You'll feel better.

Tips for Self-Care

S **Sleep**, eat and exercise. Eat the right foods in the right quantities. Sleep more. Move a little each day, even if exercise is not really your thing. Walk a dog. Sign up for a 5K in the park. Join a dance class.

E **Engage** with your imagination. Write, draw, journal, paint. Check out local community centers for free classes. Try a new hobby or discover a new passion. Go to the library and check out a book or a movie. Listen to podcasts.

L **Love** yourself. Say affirmations like "I love and appreciate you," "You're beautiful," "You are worthy and deserve greatness," "You are the most important person in my life." Take a break from school, homework, extracurricular activities, your job and any other stressors when you need to. Take a long shower, paint your nails, style your hair, or give yourself a facial. Go for a walk, dance, or sing to the mirror.

F **Find** inspiration. Meditate. Stop and breathe before and after you brush your teeth, or before a test at school, or while listening to music. Explore what spirituality means to you. Attend a religious or spiritual service. Read scripture or inspirational sayings.

C **Connect** with friends, family and those in need. Cook or bake together. FaceTime or Skype with someone. Create a goal together and support each other in reaching it. Walk dogs at an animal shelter. Tutor kids younger than you. Raise money for a cause. Help out with a political campaign. Do something for someone else and make yourself happier too.

A **Adopt** a schedule. Make professional self-care appointments when needed. Do your homework so you don't fall behind. Clean your room and do your chores. Attend to important tasks. Plan your financial life. Schedule your self-care!

R **Release** emotions. Watch a sad/funny movie or episode. Talk to a spiritual leader or therapist. Sing at the top of your lungs. Scream into your pillow. Caress your own body.

E **Enjoy** nature. Take a walk or go on a hike. Grow some vegetables or plant a window box. Visit a garden center or a nursery. Go outside; leave your phone behind. Do outdoor social events instead of social media. Rather than mindlessly surfing the net, body surf at the beach.

A Note to Parents

I hope you thought of a bajillion more topics to talk about with your daughter. We don't have to be experts to love our daughters. We just have to be willing to listen, to communicate, to speak about those things we have always known, and to research those things we know nothing about. Your daughter has so much to teach you, right? She has so much to say. Sometimes she won't know that she needs you. Sometimes she won't want to share a secret because she won't know where to start... or whether you will still love her afterwards.

Watch for the truths about your daughter that were so apparent when she was a baby: She's hungry. She's scared. She's cold or hot or wet. She's sad or mad or happy. You knew then, and you haven't lost it yet... although you will feel like you've lost it sometimes! When she cries, find out why, and don't be afraid to cry with her. There were many things I wished my mama would have told me, but there were many things my mama didn't know. And when she did reach out to me in her own way, sometimes I wasn't ready to listen.

When all else fails, you have your heart and your soul and your love intimately connected to that young woman you are raising. My mama didn't have to tell me that her love and soul were intimately connected to me. She wouldn't have used those words anyway. She showed me many of the most important lessons, and I felt her deep caring and concern. I am grateful, Mama. Thank you.

Acknowledgments

The first draft of this book was, indeed, shitty, Anne Lamott. I owe deepest gratitude to my writing coach and first content editor, Marni Freedman, who helped me take the stories of my teen years and morph them into a book that teens could relate to. I am thankful to my first ever writing group, Writer's Elements: Ellen Hohenstein (Earth), Parminder Randhawa (Sky), Cristina Malo (Fire), Elizabeth Macias-Meade (Wind), and me (Water—because of the many tears I've shed).

I am grateful to Cali Linfor, who told me I could be a writer if I wanted to be. On the day I retired, she said, "So let's talk about your future as a writer." She critiqued my first submission after retirement, "Working and Walking the Boulevard" which led to publication in *Sunshine Noir II*.

I am grateful to San Diego Writers Ink, who introduced me to Tami Greenwood and Marni Freedman, and started me on my path to be a writer. In those rooms, I met aspiring writers who became future critique groups. I cannot possibly remember all of their names, but I am grateful. I am grateful to my Beta readers: Franciene Lehmann, Tania Pryputniewicz, and Julie Needham. I am grateful to Ellen Hohenstein for fact checking any chapter that contained medical information. I am grateful to Donna Agins, who lovingly and assertively helped me get my research and chapters organized so that I could see what I was doing. I am grateful to Jean Di Carlo-Wagner, who gave me her art studio for a week when I needed it the most.

This book would only be my teen stories from the 1960s and 1970s if it were not for the current teens I interviewed and a few adults whose teen stories were so compelling, they could not be left out. Thank you to teachers Ellen Hohenstein and Michael Heu for allowing me to present my project to their students. Their students' stories, along with journal entries and after-school chats with high school students I taught for many years, provided the "Your Story" portion of each chapter. For their words, their insights, and their bravery, I will be forever indebted. I cannot list their names here because I want to protect their anonymity, but they know who they are, and I hope they know how important their stories will be to hundreds of young women (and older women who are still trying to heal the teen within).

I will be forever grateful to Acorn Publishing and all of the wonderful folk who work for and with Holly Kammier and Jessica Therrien to make authors' dreams come to life. Molly Lewis edited the content until it was everything I wanted it to be, but couldn't do alone. Debra Kennedy made sure every line was perfect and formatted the book for printing. Jennifer Silva Redmond proofread the final copy. Cami Hensley helped me get the book out into the worlds of social media and online book sellers. Thanks to Damonza and Lindsey Salatka for my cover design. Lindsey also designed my website and became my confidant, teacher, cheerleader, and the receiver of my tears.

Last, but absolutely not least, I am grateful to my family. My sisters—Peggy, Julie, and Cindy—for listening, giving feedback, gifting writing journals, and acknowledging my fears. My children: Jesse and Holly, for spending hours in creative conversations and helping me with my technology nightmares; Luke and Nicole, for creating logos, and teaching me about apps, social media, and other tech voodoo; Noah and Jolene, for giving me perspective on how different every teen and family experience is. Special thanks to Noah, who allowed me to include some of his journey when it overlapped with mine. My husband, Tom, for allowing me to share his story as part of my story. It was a brave and loving thing to do. My grandchildren—Nora, Eli, Ian and Sophia—for taking me out of writing into the joy of silliness and play. Little Georgia, born only six months ago; our story is still to be written.

There are so many more who have had an influence on my decision to be a writer. I cannot possibly list them all. They are my parents, my grandparents, my teachers, my mentors. They are random folks I met at writing conferences who gave me a kind word of encouragement. They are writers in my different groups and even in my family who showed me that it's possible to finish and share a book because they did it first. They are all the women and men in my recovery groups who love me and keep me sane, especially my BFF, who had to talk me off the ledge more than once. They are my sponsors, my sponsees, and my therapist. They are all the writers who have come before me, and the muses that come with them. This is my list of gratitude.

Resources

Sources for Support for You or Others in Need:

Online Sites, HelpLines & Tips, Organizations

On Friendship & Bullying—Chapter 3

www.stopbullying.gov

www.connectsafely.org

If you or a friend is being bullied, talk to an adult you trust. (See a teacher, school counselor, school principal, or school superintendent.)

If the person is at immediate risk, call 911

If you or a friend is feeling hopeless and thinking of suicide, contact the National Suicide Prevention Lifeline or call 1-800-273-TALK (8255)

On Stress & Healthy Living—Chapter 6

National Suicide Prevention Lifeline: 1-800-273-8255 (TALK)

Warmline (an alternative to a crisis line run by peers): https://warmline.org

On LGBTQIA Resources—Chapter 11

GLSEN (Gay, Lesbian & Straight Education Network): www.glsen.org

It Gets Better Project (For LGBTQ+ Youth): https://itgetsbetter.org

The Evolve Project: https://theevolveproject.org

The Trevor Project (Saving Young LGBTQ Lives): www.thetrevorproject.org

Crisis Lines for LGBTQ:

The Trevor Project: 1-866-488-7386

National Suicide Prevention Lifeline: 1-800-273-8255 (TALK)

Trans Lifeline Hotline: 1-877-565-8860; https://translifeline.org

National Runaway Safeline: 1-800-786-2929 (RUNAWAY)
www.1800runaway.org

On Sex, STDs & Birth Control—Chapters 13 and 14

Planned Parenthood: www.plannedparenthood.org; 1-800-230-PLAN

Centers for Disease Control and Prevention: www.cdc.gov; 1-800-232-4636

U.S. Department of Health and Human Services, Office of Population Affairs (Title X Family Planning, Teen Pregnancy Prevention Program, Pregnancy Assistance Fund, and Embryo Adoption Awareness Program): https://opa.hhs.gov; 1-877-696-6775

On Abuse & Violence—Chapters 16 and 17

National Resource Center on Domestic Violence (NRCDV): https://nrcdv.org

National Domestic Violence Hotline: 1-800-799-SAFE (7233)

Love is Respect (Empowering Youth to End Dating Abuse): www.loveisrespect.org

Love is Respect National Dating Abuse Helpline: 1-866-331-9474

On Addiction & Alcohol—Chapter 21

Alcoholics Anonymous (AA): www.aa.org; 1-844-335-2408

Al-Anon (For Families and Friends of Alcoholics): https://al-anon.org; Toll-free meeting line: 1-888-425-2666

Alateen Teen Corner (Al-Anon for Teens): https://al-anon.org

*Permissions Received by **Al-Anon Family Group Headquarters, Inc.** for teen quotes in the "Your Story" section of Chapter 21. Credit lines and Disclaimers:*

- From ***How Al-Anon Works for Families and Friends of Alcoholics***, copyright 1995, 2008 by Al-Anon Family Group Headquarters, Inc. Reprinted by permission of Al-Anon Family Group Headquarters, Inc. Permission to reprint these excerpts does not mean that Al-Anon Family Group Headquarters, Inc. has reviewed or approved the contents of this publication, or that Al-Anon Family Group Headquarters, Inc. necessarily agrees with the views expressed herein. Al-Anon is a program of recovery for families and friends of alcoholics—use of these excerpts in any non Al-Anon context does not imply endorsement or affiliation by Al-Anon.

- From ***Al-Anon Faces Alcoholism*** 2013 magazine, copyright 2012 by Al-

---

Books Mentioned

In Chapter 6
The 60 Second Fix: The Brain-Changing Toolkit That Stops Unwanted Habits and Starts Surprising Joy by Regalena Melrose, Ph.D.

In Chapter 8
Roadtrip Nation: A Guide to Discovering Your Path in Life chronicles the PBS series and is published by Ballantine Books.

In Chapter 16
Dreamland by Sarah Dessen: Caitlin dates Rogerson Biscoe, who is handsome, sensitive, and mysterious. He keeps Caitlin in a dreamland from which she can't seem to break free even after the dream turns into a nightmare of abuse.

Breathing Underwater by Alex Flinn: Sent to counseling for hitting his girlfriend, Caitlin, and ordered to keep a journal, sixteen-year-old Nick recounts his relationship with Caitlin, examines his controlling behavior and anger, and describes living with his abusive father.

Note About Resources Used During Research

I researched and listened to internet articles, YouTube videos, and TED Talks written and presented by experts, parents, and teens. As I listened and read, I took notes and wrapped my brain around the issues. My purpose in using all of the available avenues on the internet was not to quote experts on reliable sites. I wanted to hear from teens, their parents, and yes, of course, experts. But I was more interested in patterns than in facts or professional opinions. After researching each chapter, I had a sense for common threads, trends, and statistics. I only used information that all of my sources agreed upon, whether a teen in her bedroom on YouTube or a Ph.D. Finally, I put that information into easy-to-understand charts, acronyms, acrostics, or diagrams so that teens and their parents would be able to access answers that would help them.

I am grateful to all of the sites, studies, and reports that have done extensive work on all of the issues discussed in this book. Some statistics from sites such as CDC or Pew Research, for example, are included and the study is mentioned. Other than statistics, I did not directly quote any information from the many sources I read.

Note About the Student Stories (Your Story)

Students were contacted in one of three ways: 1) Through class presentations with their teachers, 2) Through personal contact with past students, or 3) From journal entries of past students. I presented my project to over 100 high school students. Thirty of those students submitted a one-page story on one of the topics I gave them, and I conducted over thirty interviews by phone or face to face. Students who were still in high school or were minors were required to have a permission slip signed by their parents. All student names were changed to protect their anonymity.

About the Author

Nancy Mae Johnson is an author, mentor, educator, and advocate with more than 20 years of experience listening, learning, and guiding teens through their life stories. After surviving her own tumultuous high school life and teen marriage, Johnson entered college at age 32 and dedicated the rest of her adult life to being a teen advocate.

Johnson graduated *summa cum laude* from SDSU with a BS in English Literature and an MA in Secondary Education. She taught English within a Visual and Performing Arts Academy until her retirement in 2014. Today, she advocates for teens in her role as Director of Teen Programming for the San Diego Writers Festival. She mentors teens in local high schools as they write their stories for KidsWrite! San Diego, and shares weekly with Alateens in recovery.

Nancy lives in La Mesa, California, and finds joy in her husband, children, grandchildren, her garden, and her dog, Phoebe. Visit Nancy at nancypantsjohnson.com to read her blog, follow her school visits with teens, and be an advocate yourself by donating one book to one teen in the inner city. You can also find her on Facebook @ nancyjohnson3766 or Instagram @ #nancypantsjohnson.